RICH CHURCH —
POOR CHURCH?

ORBIS BOOKS   MARYKNOLL   NEW YORK

RICH CHURCH — POOR CHURCH?

SOME BIBLICAL PERSPECTIVES

Enzo Gatti

Translated by Matthew J. O'Connell

Originally published as *Colui Che Sa Il Dolore Dell'Uomo,*
2nd edition, Copyright 1973 by Editrice Missionarie Italiane

Copyright © 1974, Orbis Books, Maryknoll, New York 10545

Library of Congress Catalog Card Number 74-77432

ISBN 0-88344-437-2

Manufactured in the United States of America

CONTENTS

PREFACE TO THE SECOND EDITION

The biblical message is explosive: when it is preached to the poor it can lead to the destruction of any and every oppressive structure, whether political, social, economic, cultural, or religious. Provided that it is accepted for what it is and allowed to speak its own language, it is a leaven of liberation and humanization. Christ constantly seeks to be born again of poverty and virginity.

This little incident from my own recent experience struck me as rather significant. One of my teaching colleagues was asked to write an article on the beatitudes. He walked agitatedly down the corridor where the faculty lives, asking exegete and systematic theologian, moralist and liturgist: "What on earth does 'Blessed are the poor' mean? Who are these blessed poor?" Because we have conducted learned discussions on the Bible and left it in the hands of specialists, we have it nicely covered over with a layer of intellectual refinements and exegetical tinsel. We have turned it into a work of chiefly cultural interest—unless we have gone a step further and more or less consciously manipulated it for our own comfort or advantage.

If only we will strip away the robes we orthodox, comfortable Christians have put on the Bible, if only we will let it emerge from our sacristies, then the scriptural Christ will once again speak to the poor, and his words will become a liberating force, challenging every form of oppression. Only the poor can restore to God's word the resonances of liberation that are native to it. They are the natural ground in which that word takes root and flowers; they provide the atmosphere it needs if its full meaning is to emerge.

Since God's word, and it alone, is the only reality that is the source of creative innovation, renewal, and liberation in history—the only utterly new thing that has penetrated into our world and the only power capable of transforming it—the poor are the world's salvation. And since God's Church comes to birth, and can only come to birth, out of God's word as continually preached, accepted, and interiorized by the power of the Spirit, the poor are the Church's salvation, too, the ones on whom its survival depends.

The desire which led to the writing of the following pages was that of presenting in biblical terms the theme of the *Church's vocation to the poor,* which is the same as saying the *Christian's vocation to mission*: God's call to Christians to bear witness to his offer of salvation and proclaim it to the man of today who has not yet encountered Christ or entered into dialogue with him. To avoid misconceptions and useless rhetoric as far as possible, I have tried to present, on the one hand, the One who calls—his demands, his preferences, his lines of action, his mode of intervention in our human situation. On the other, I have set out to describe those who have first claim on his invitation and attention—the privileged recipients of his saving activity, the areas of human existence to which he prefers to turn, the citizens of his kingdom.

Yahweh, the God of the Bible, enters on the stage of history as a revolutionary, liberating force. In the first phase of his activity, he frees Israel from Egyptian domination; in the second (still limited to the Israelite people), he frees the exploited from the exploiter; in the third (the last great historical experience of Israel), he once more delivers his people, this time from Babylonian oppression. The picture that emerges from his interventions seems to be this: the God of Israel is a God of freedom who challenges every form of human slavery; a God who treats all men equally, defends man against man, and thus in the most radical way promotes the liberation and humanization of the person.

These characteristics, which are already evident in the pages of the Old Testament, become fully clear in Christ, who is God's definitive Word of salvation to mankind. Christ is, beyond all others, the one who is called to be

God's representative in the world; he is God's mission to man and the model for anyone who undertakes to communicate, by his own life and word, the salvation which the God of Christ offers to man in his totality.

Christ comes to us as the definitive and radical fulfillment of God's promises to mankind. His saving word is of its nature meant for all men: it embraces the individual in the totality of his being and mankind in its entirety. It is precisely this radically universal bearing of Christ's offer of salvation that makes him a judgment on the world and on every religious society which lays claim to his name.

The community of those who believe in Christ, the Son whose conquest over death and human limitations has been definitive, is transformed by Christ's Spirit into a missionary community of salvation. Its characteristics are communion, service, and the positive and explicit proclamation of the Gospel message. No consideration of the vocation of the Christian as an individual person can leave this communal setting and these elements of ecclesial community out of account.

This book lays no claim to be anything more than a presentation of some points in Scripture which will stimulate reflection on the missionary dimension of the Christian vocation. Today there is a crying need that the Gospel should be preached to the poor: the choice made once and for all on their behalf opens up immense possibilities for the living of the Christian vocation in our contemporary secularized world. At the same time, the real conditions in which missionary activity and the missionary vocation must be carried out today require that the institutes which claim to be the most concrete and effective expression of the missionary thrust in the ecclesial communities should adopt new positions and accept revisions of their activity that are both courageous and responsive to the times.

These pages have grown chiefly out of dialogue with groups of young people and with missionaries as such who are already involved in the social, economic, and political spheres. The book is intended primarily for such people, with the hope that in frank and open communal discussion they may penetrate more deeply into its thoughts, clarify them, and apply them in concrete ways.

1

LET MY PEOPLE GO

WHERE AUTHORITY AND POWER
BECOME SUPERFLUOUS

The Old Testament has no direct concern with missionary activity, for Christ alone opens the gates of salvation to mankind as a whole. Israel's religious experience is but an age-long, laborious journey towards the clear, final word of salvation which God speaks to mankind when he decides to inaugurate the final, definitive stage of human history. Yet this same religious experience of Israel is indispensable to us if we are to understand, at least in an initial, sketchy way, the manner in which the God of the Bible intervenes in human affairs, and the kind of salvation that God brings to mankind and makes fully and definitively clear in Christ.

The God of Israel intervenes in his people's history in very characteristic ways. His action shows certain constants that are unmistakable. He is a God who is not conditioned by the cycles of nature and the cosmos; he relates himself immediately to man and man's situation; he is concerned with the total being of man, whether as individual or as member of an ethnic group with its social, political, religious, and economic relationships. This God is in no way jealous of man's freedom and dignity. On the contrary: to this God we can say, "You have made him [man] little less than the angels, and crowned him with glory and honor. You have given him rule over the works of your hands, putting all things under his feet" (Ps. 8:6-7).

This concern for man and for a hominized world, this intention, ever more explicitly manifested, to make man free and to defend that freedom against any divinity or pseudo-divinity that challenges it, against any obstacles to its unfolding, make of Yahweh, Israel's God, a unique God. He is "the God of man," not the God of nature or of structures or of the king or the priests or the powerful.

Since he is the God of men he is very much in earnest with regard to man's problems and aspirations. He will intervene unfailingly whenever man's innate requirements for economic, social, political, or religious freedom are put in doubt; whenever man's freedom from hunger and oppression of any kind—from the religious idols which alienate him, from the forces within himself, and above all the limitations imposed by sin and death—seems doomed to remain an unattainable, utopian ideal. Yahweh does not hesitate to become the faithful, tireless, travelling companion of man and of the people he initially chose that he might "show his face to them." He accompanies them along the roads and through the deserts they must traverse to reach the "promised" land where God is really God and man can therefore be truly man (Jürgen Moltmann); on that journey towards the realm of freedom which Ernst Bloch, the modern panegyrist of liberty, describes as follows:

> Where authority and power become superfluous, domination over persons is exchanged for administration of things. When freedom to seek profit is replaced by freedom from profit, and when leisure and the Muses are joined to freedom, we will be able to solve our most important problems. Mankind's desire for light grows ever greater through the history that runs from the prophets to Jesus.[1]

THE RISKS OF FREEDOM

> *The first step towards freedom is to suffer under slavery and find it intolerable. One who resigns himself to a passive acceptance of destiny, whether his own or that of the other "citizens of Egypt," cannot encounter Yahweh, the God who brings freedom.*[2]

Anyone who reads the Bible of the Hebrews and compares it with the "bibles" of their neighbors and Semitic brothers is struck by one fact. The "gods of the nations" (as Israel called the divinities of contemporary peoples) have no creative imagination; their interventions and actions can be fully anticipated; they do and say, for the most part, what the political and religious powers-that-be do and say. Yahweh, on the contrary, is unpredictable; he is unwilling to be the sacralized reflection of human throne and altar.

Even in the Bible (we are speaking for the moment of the Old Testament) not everything is the word of this very original God; we do find things there that might be found in other religions. Even the Bible gives evidence of various schools and currents of thought and concern. Even in the Bible we find traces of an effort to reformulate the earlier traditions and reduce them to a common theocratic message. (This was the work of the priestly tradition, which arose quite late in the history of Israelite literature, after the Exile.) Not every presentation of Yahweh sounds the note of a battle-cry against oppression or of prophetic inspiration to another flight from Pharaoh.

However, it is the Christ-event which must serve as the norm in all interpretation of Israel's millennial religious experience; and if we read the Old Testament in this light, we find in it a subversive message of liberation which addresses itself to the condition of the poor and oppressed of every age. It emerges especially in the prophets and the book of Exodus. Let us begin with Israel's first and constitutive historical

6

experience: the rebellion against Pharaoh and the flight from Egypt.

When and how did Israel encounter its God? It met him while in a situation which, humanly speaking, was hopeless; in a situation of economic, social, political, and religious alienation. The people was enslaved in Egypt by a power which, though providing its daily bread, took away its freedom and prevented it from being a people, the people of Yahweh, God of freedom and humanization.

> Then a new king . . . came to power in Egypt. He said to his subjects, "Look how numerous and powerful the Israelite people are growing, more so than we ourselves! Come, let us deal shrewdly with them to stop their increase. . . . " Accordingly, taskmasters were set in power over the Israelites to oppress them with forced labor. Thus they had to build for Pharaoh the supply cities of Pithom and Rameses. Yet the more they were oppressed, the more they multiplied and spread. The Egyptians, then, dreaded the Israelites and reduced them to cruel slavery, making life bitter for them with hard work in mortar and brick and all kinds of field work—the whole cruel fate of slaves (Exod. 1:8-14).

That is the picture we are given at the beginning of the book of Exodus, which then goes on to tell of the struggle between the forces of freedom: Yahweh and his messengers, and the forces of slavery: Pharaoh, his gods and magicians, his armies and wealth.

7

"Egypt was like Auschwitz" was the comment of a Jewish student. The author—or better, the editor—of Exodus has gathered and combined more or less ancient traditions (all of them, in any event, much later than the events narrated); his primary intention is to say that Yahweh is a God who can free man from even the most oppressive slavery. The worse the slavery in which man—individual or in community—finds himself, the greater the salvific power the God of the Bible manifests.

Implicit in these same pages of the Bible is another very important statement: the first—and indispensable—step towards freedom is to suffer under slavery and find it intolerable. Some people fear the risks involved in freedom and seek to avoid them. Others are simply indifferent to freedom, feel it is not worth struggling for. Still others are even anxious to trade in their freedom for an easy, cowardly peace: actually they are abdicating their manhood. None of these various kinds of men are capable of being followers of Yahweh, the God of human freedom.

THE GOD OF THE BIBLE:
A GOD OF FREEDOM

The ID card of the God of the Bible bears these words: "I am always ready to intervene and free-and-save the man who is a

8

slave and knows he is a slave; that is, the man who is open to receive my freedom-bringing word."

The biblical narrative goes on to describe the enslavement of the Hebrews in greater detail. Their newborn male children are to be killed, for fear that this people might increase and acquire sufficient numbers and strength to risk rebellion. At this point Moses is "miraculously" saved, for he is to become the leader of his people. Later on, Moses meets the God of Israel. Yahweh introduces himself: *I am who am* (Exod. 3:14). "I am the one who is ready to act, with the same changeless fidelity and will to save that I showed in the past to your fathers, Abraham, Isaac, and Jacob. I am the God of the promises, which I will not fail to carry out. I ask only that you have faith in me. I am ready to irrupt into history, to intervene with my saving power in any area of human life where men are in need or in any kind of slavery." (This is the interpretation which contemporary exegetes think most probable for the translation of this famous biblical statement as: *I will be what I will be.*) Thus: "My intervention will far outstrip your hopes. I will save you, whatever the resistance of forces opposed to freedom. Though they may be greater than human imagination can grasp, I will prevail against them. I am the God of your freedom and your future."

9

From the very beginning the God of Israel makes his intentions and preferences known: he is on the side of the oppressed and is well aware of their situation. It might even be said that he seeks weakness out in order to show his saving power, slavery to show his liberating might, the desert (geographic symbol of human poverty, especially in the second Exodus) to show his creative, life-giving energy.

God presents himself straightway as a God of freedom. By following him—and only so—Israel will win political, social, and spiritual freedom. "I have witnessed the affliction of my people in Egypt and have heard their cry of complaint against their slave-drivers, so I know well what they are suffering. . . . The cry of the Israelites has reached me, and I have truly noted that the Egyptians are oppressing them. Come, now! I will send you to Pharaoh to lead my people, the Israelites, out of Egypt" (Exod. 3:7-10).

The Bible thus shows us that Yahweh's first involvement with his people is involvement in an act of liberation that takes them from Egypt to the promised land by way of the desert. Egypt—desert—promised land; kingdom of slavery—covenant with God—kingdom of freedom: such is the basic pattern according to which the God of freedom deals with his people. It is a dynamic pattern of liberation and freedom.

The God of Israel will always be the God

who frees man from the "house of slavery" (as Egypt is often called in the Bible) in order to make him a partner and to lead him to true freedom. On the primitive level, Israel's experience of freedom was concerned with the possibility of moving about in space. But Egypt, the desert, and the promised land are soon transformed and radicalized into symbols of slavery, the way to freedom, and freedom itself. The Exodus becomes a form-giving pattern for all the basic Israelite experiences of salvation; it becomes, for us, one of the theological categories required for reading the Bible. Its capacity as a symbol and its native fruitfulness are such that it can express ever deeper and more universal experiences, as well as ever new manifestations of God's liberating power at work in history.

The Exodus becomes a pattern of salvation even in the Old Testament. Israel describes and relives every experience of salvation in the light of the Exodus; it appeals to this model of deliverance at all the decisive moments in its historical progress; it introduces it into its professions of faith as the first and basic article, that which best expresses its faith in the God of freedom. Here is the Israelite creed:

> My father was a wandering Aramean who went down to Egypt with a small household and lived there as an alien. But there he became a nation, great, strong and numerous. When the Egyptians maltreated and oppressed us, imposing hard labor

upon us, we cried to the Lord, the God of our fathers, and he heard our cry and saw our affliction, our toil and our oppression. He brought us out of Egypt with his strong hand and outstretched arm, with terrifying power, with signs and wonders; and bringing us into this country, he gave us this land flowing with milk and honey (Deut. 26:5-9).

THE PROPHETS CRY OUT
AGAINST OPPRESSION

The prophet of Yahweh involves himself and his God directly in the conflict of oppressor and oppressed. His God descends into the fight (bringing his prophet with him) on the side of the oppressed.

The Egyptian situation is repeated in the history of Israel after the people has become a sedentary nation of farmers in Canaan. Though in Palestine Israel may no longer be forced to make bricks, the Egyptian rulers and other oppressive forces have not ceased to exist: only the name has changed. Life threatens to become even harsher. Even within God's people the laws of social stratification create the division and dialectical opposition between rich and poor. The wealth of the few produces even here,

12

gradually and with increasing differentiation in external life-style, the poverty of the many. In this situation it is the prophets who bring Yahweh's clear and piercing words of judgment in favor of the poor against the ruling class of oppressors.

The striking thing about the prophets is that, unlike the prophets of other religions, they do not automatically preach obedience to the established order; nor do they confine themselves to predicting destined events that square with the long-range programs of the political authorities. Instead we find them in constant opposition to the status quo within which they live and work for peace and social equality. Even more surprising, their greatest concern is to defend not the rights of the One who sent them but those of the human person.

AMOS: with Hosea, Amos is the first prophet whose oracles have come down to us, though they were gathered and arranged only after his death. He lived during the reign of Jeroboam II, King of Israel (the Northern Kingdom) from 784 to 744 B.C. It was a time of economic prosperity, owing to the unusual peace Israel enjoyed despite being a buffer state between two great powers, Egypt and Assyria. The oracles of Amos present Yahweh as the God of the poor, even if this means pitting him not only against the rich but also against the political and ecclesiastical hierarchies. Amos' message is one of war upon throne and altar and of peace to the dwellers in thatched huts:

Hear and bear witness against the house of Jacob, says the Lord God, the God of Hosts:
> *On the day when I punish Israel for his crimes,*
> *I will visit also the altars of Bethel:*
> *the horns of the altar shall be broken off*
> *and fall to the ground.*
> *Then will I strike the winter house*
> *and the summer house;*
> *the ivory apartments shall be ruined,*
> *and their many rooms shall be no more,*
> *says the Lord* (Amos 3:13-15).

Bethel was the official sanctuary of the kingdom. The chief priest, Amaziah, was of course not pleased with such preaching, for it represented a danger to Jeroboam. The chief priest therefore commanded Amos: "Off with you!... Never again prophesy in Bethel; for it is the king's sanctuary and a royal temple" (Amos 7:12; 7:10-17 is the only autobiographical section in the whole book). But Amos was not afraid to attack the religious hierarchy which had become the servant of political power. He accuses them all: "They sell the just man for silver, and the poor man for a pair of sandals. They trample the heads of the weak into the dust of the earth" (Amos 2:6-7).

With Amos as his mouthpiece, Yahweh proclaims that he will abide in the midst of his

14

people only if they "seek the good of the brethren" in their lives.

> *Therefore because you have trampled upon the weak*
> *and exacted of them levies of grain,*
> *though you have built houses of hewn stone,*
> *you shall not live in them! . . .*
> *Yes, I know how many are your crimes,*
> *how grievous your sins:*
> *oppressing the just, accepting bribes,*
> *repelling the needy at the gate! . . .*
> *Seek good and not evil,*
> *that you may live;*
> *then truly will the Lord, the God of hosts,*
> *be with you as you claim!* (Amos 4:11-15)

It is evident, of course, that religion is not automatically and inevitably something that exerts a positive influence. Both sociologically and psychologically, it is a phenomenon capable of ambiguity and ambivalence: it can be good or evil, depending on the meaning its practitioners attach to it. A sure criterion of its authenticity is that it stimulates the person to greater maturity and increases his capacity for service in the interests of his brother's freedom. Yet it can frequently become the means of silencing one's conscience. To give to temple, church, parish, or charitable institution what might better be devoted to the urgent needs of the poor can be an act of social injustice. Amos has hard words for that kind of religiosity; even the pious ladies who faithfully visit the temple are not spared:

Hear this word, women of the mountain of Samaria,
    you cows of Bashan,
you who oppress the weak
    and abuse the needy;
who say to your lords,
    "Bring drink for us!"
The Lord God has sworn by his holiness:
    Truly the days are coming upon you
when they shall drag you away with hooks. . . .

Come to Bethel and sin,
    to Gilgal, and sin the more;
each morning bring your sacrifices,
    every third day, your tithes;
burn leavened food as a thanksgiving sacrifice,
    proclaim publicly your freewill offerings,
for so you love to do, O men of Israel,
    says the Lord God (Amos 4:1-5).

In the religious cultures of the time we find a widespread misconception of God, as men set out to defend the rights of the divinity while ignoring the rights of man. More simply: they give priority to the rights of their god over the rights of man and the struggle for social justice. In our own day, the existence of immense, barrackslike religious complexes (churches and religious structures in general) and the perpetual program for church-building in various dioceses are but one obvious example of the same attitude. The God of the prophet Amos, the God of the prophets generally, seems to be saying something else. He seems to be saying, quite simply: I do not want you to defend my rights, real or imaginary; I want you to struggle and expend your energies in advancing the rights of the poor and the oppressed:

> *I hate, I spurn your feasts,*
> > *I take no pleasure in your solemnities;*
> *your cereal offerings I will not accept,*
> > *nor consider your stall-fed peace offerings.*
> *Away with your noisy songs!*
> > *I will not listen to the melodies of your harps.*
> *But if you would offer me holocausts,*
> > *then let justice surge like water,*
> > *and goodness like an unfailing stream*
> (Amos 5:21-24).

MISCONCEIVING THE ROLE
OF THE LITURGY

Even today it is still quite possible to try to live a full Christian life in ways which have no resemblance to that authentic renewal of which Scripture speaks. Even today we can see widespread evidence of the attempt, though in more subtle forms, to make cultic compensation, as it were, for the inadequacies of our lives in relation to our neighbors.

What we have called "misconceiving the

17

role of the liturgy" can flourish even today, when too much importance is attached to liturgical reform. More specifically: when the impression is given that there can be an authentic expression of ecclesial Christian life, in the form of communal worship, which is not based on an authentic experience of Christian community living. One of the commonest temptations of religious man is involved here, namely that of a misconceived sacralization. By this we mean the restriction of dialogue with God to fixed times and places, so that his influence is automatically excluded from the rest of human life and activity. God then becomes man's tool; his absolute and unlimited sovereignty over man is restricted; his unique, authentic reality as the God of man is emptied of content. Thus God is reduced to an "idol" that is at man's disposal; his interventions and requirements can be programmed, as it were, by man.

Trying to love God without loving our neighbor: that is the temptation which can turn religion into a type of evasion and alienation. For God, after all, is invisible, while our neighbor is terribly real and demanding.

In order, then, to avoid all equivocation, the God of the prophets seems to want to eliminate all rivalry between himself and men. Not only that; through his prophet's word he makes it impossible for anyone to monopolize him and make of him nothing but a sacralized, legitimating image of the powers that be; he is not there for man to use.

ISAIAH: the greatest of the Israelite prophets. He exercised his prophetic activity in the political, social, and religious sphere from about 740 to 690 B.C., in the kingdom of Judah, at a time when his nation was passing through very important internal and external political changes. His oracles are to be found especially in chapters 1-23 and 28-33 of the book that bears his name. (Chapters 36-39 contain biographical information and form a kind of historical appendix.)

One of Isaiah's compositions, perhaps the best piece of poetry he produced, deals precisely with our subject. Yahweh is afraid that he is being worshipped at the expense of the poor; that devotion to him involves neglect of the concrete duty of seeking justice; that the practice of religion is an escape from social tasks rather than a stimulus to their fulfillment. Here is what the prophet says:

> Hear the word of the Lord,
>   princes of Sodom!
> Listen to the instruction of our God,
>   people of Gomorrah!
> What care I for the number of your sacrifices?
>   says the Lord.
> I have had enough of whole-burnt rams
>   and fat of fatlings;
> in the blood of calves, lambs and goats

19

I find no pleasure.
When you come in to visit me,
   who asks these things of you?
Trample my courts no more!
   Bring no more worthless offerings;
   your incense is loathsome to me.
New moon and sabbath, calling of assemblies,
   octaves with wickedness: these I cannot bear.
Your new moons and festivals I detest;
   they weigh me down, I tire of the load.
When you spread out your hands,
   I close my eyes to you;
though you pray the more,
   I will not listen.
Your hands are full of blood!
   Wash yourselves clean!
Put away your misdeeds from before my eyes;
   cease doing evil; learn to do good.
Make justice your aim; redress the wronged,
   hear the orphan's plea, defend the widow
(Isa. 1:10-17).[3]

The orphan and widow are types of those
strata of society which are the most neglected,
exploited, and helpless. Yahweh cannot bear that
men should think of him while forgetting the
oppressed. Very often (and this is one of the
things that strikes us most forcibly in reading
them) the God of the biblical prophets prefers,
and even opposes, the interests of justice and the
poor to those of the temple and religion.[4]

HOSEA, contemporary of Amos, provides an
interesting passage (4:1-4) in which the "knowl-

edge of God" is identified with love of neighbor. The same thought is taken up in the First Letter of John (2:3-11).

JEREMIAH saw the tragic signs of the fall of Israel and Jerusalem and of the total destruction of the kingdom of Judah (which occurred in 587).

The following passages of Jeremiah are pertinent to our concerns:

6:6-14: against every kind of violence.

7:1-24: Yahweh rejects the attempt to compensate by temple worship for the injustices done to the brethren. He sharply condemns those who faithfully attend the temple and invoke the Lord's name there, while scorning his commandments in everyday life.

9:1-8   condemns injustice.

Psalm 50 provides another eloquent example of the authentic religion which the central biblical tradition seeks to foster. It is a special kind of psalm, for the person who speaks in it is not man at prayer but God, accusing his people of infidelity to the covenant.

(Psalm 51 is the people's answer; they ask for pardon and pray for the Spirit to come and make them new.)

After a description of the cultic theophany

of Yahweh (1-4) and a summons from God to the people to stand trial (5-6), Psalm 50 launches into God's accusation against the people (7-21). Within this discourse there is, first of all, a sharp rejection of attempts to win God over through the cultus (7-15) and, then, a clear denunciation of Israel's sins (16-21). This last is the passage that interests us most. In it we find a list of sins, not against God, but against the neighbor. Fidelity to God thus means fidelity to one's brother. The psalm ends with a kind of final peroration (22-23), an invitation to recognize and do the will of this "God of man."

GOD'S BREAD TO FEED THE HUNGRY

Perhaps the prophetic message requires the Christian community (dioceses, parishes, religious institutes, and churches generally) to effect a radical revision in its ways of operating, planning, spending, and living.

The words of the prophets are more relevant to us than may at first sight appear. Today, as we have suggested, instead of the fat of fatlings and whole-burnt offerings of bulls and lambs they would speak of immense buildings erected for worship and of an excessive concern given to planning and building houses for God.

What the Christian God seeks is a house he can share with man—a house found not in Jerusalem or on Mount Gerazim, but only in man's heart and in his communion with his brothers. Where two or three are gathered in God's name he is present.[5]

This brief hint is enough for our purpose, for our primary intention is to invite the reader to reflect. I would like to end with a passage from the New Testament:

> It happened that he was walking through standing grain on the sabbath, and his disciples began to pull off heads of grain as they went along. At this the Pharisees protested: "Look! Why do they do a thing not permitted on the sabbath?" He said to them: "Have you never read what David did when he was in need and he and his men were hungry? How he entered God's house in the days of Abiathar the high priest and ate the holy bread which only the priests were permitted to eat? He even gave it to his men." Then he said to them: "The sabbath was made for man, not man for the sabbath. That is why the Son of Man is lord even of the sabbath" (Mark 2:23-28)

When David was hard-pressed and hungry, he did not hesitate to enter the temple and eat the loaves which only the priests were permitted to eat. Jesus refers to this fact and comments on it, in order to make it clear that man is more precious than structures, even religious structures.

A SALVATION WHICH IS
A NEW CREATION

> *Only at the end of time will "all the ends
> of the earth . . . behold the salvation of our
> God" (Isa. 52:10), when the eschatolog-
> ical-messianic age begins in Christ, the "last
> man" (W. G. Kümmel). Then God will
> make all things new.*
>
> *The Old Testament predicts this event
> with longing anticipation.*

This prediction, the clearest cry for deliverance to be found in the Old Testament, comes
from an anonymous prophet who lived during
the last historical period of slavery which Israel
experienced: the Babylonian exile. This prophet's
songs are contained in the book of Isaiah, chapters 40-55.

Once again Israel is

A people despoiled and plundered,
   all of them trapped in holes,
   hidden away in prisons.
They are taken as booty, with no one to rescue them,
   as spoil, with no one to demand their return
(Isa. 42:22).

This time Yahweh's action is even more
surprising, inasmuch as the instrument he
chooses is not a Hebrew but a pagan king,
Cyrus:

I, the Lord, have called you for the victory of justice,
*   I have grasped you by the hand;*
I formed you, and set you
*   as a covenant of the people,*
*   a light for the nations,*
to open the eyes of the blind,
*   to bring out prisoners from confinement,*
*   and from the dungeon, those who live in darkness*
*   (Isa. 42:6-7).*

To his emissary he promises:

*   I will go before you*
*   and level the mountains;*
*   Bronze doors I will shatter,*
*   and iron bars I will snap* (Isa. 45:2).

And to the people whom he invites to come
forth from slavery:

Fear not, for I have redeemed you;
*   I have called you by name; you are mine.*
When you pass through the water, I will be with you;
*   in the rivers you shall not drown.*
When you walk through fire, you shall not be burned;
*   the flames shall not consume you.*
For I am the Lord, your God,
*   the Holy One of Israel, your savior* (Isa. 43:1-3).

The religious consciousness of Israel, which
had been tested and purified by the experience
of exile, entered into closer contact with its
God. It recognized with growing clarity that he

25

is the only God who liberates, the only one who is able to secure man's victory over all the forces that assail his freedom.

The God of this anonymous exilic prophet is a God whose interventions in human history reach ever deeper existential levels of man's being. When a man cries out to him from any of the human enslavements to which he is subject, this God can bring about ever new and more radical exoduses from the slaveries to which freedom falls prey, ever fuller triumphs over the forces of negativity and the past.

In dazzling and marvelous fashion the God of Second Isaiah stands at the edge of the abyss of nothingness and creates order out of it. With one and the same liberating power he makes water spring forth in the desert and gardens in the steppe, new generations of men from sterile elders, justice and right from the tragic human situation, and freedom from slavery:

> *Thus says the Lord who made you,*
> *your help, who formed you from the womb:*
> *Fear not, O Jacob, my servant,*
> *the darling whom I have chosen.*
> *I will pour out water upon the thirsty ground,*
> *and streams upon the dry land;*
> *I will pour out my spirit upon your offspring,*
> *and my blessing upon your descendants.*
> *They shall spring up amid the verdure*
> *like poplars beside the flowing waters.*

One shall say, "I am the Lord's,"
    another shall be named after Jacob,
and this one shall write on his hand, "The Lord's,"
    and Israel shall be his surname (Isa. 44:2-5).

God's triumphs over the chaotic waters of
the primal abyss, of the Red Sea, and of Jordan
(symbols, all of them, of the forces opposed to
human freedom) and over the "nonbeing" of the
desert are paradigms for the will-to-deliverance
of the God of the Exodus:

Awake, awake, put on strength,
    O arm of the Lord!
Awake as in the days of old,
    in ages long ago!
Was it not you who crushed Rahab,
    you who pierced the dragon?
Was it not you who dried up the sea,
    the waters of the great deep,
who made the depths of the sea into a way
    for the redeemed to pass over? (Isa. 51:9-10).

The second Exodus, more radical than the
first, shows the immense creative power of God
over cosmos and history. He effects the marvelous, the impossible, the totally new, that which
does not develop from anything in man's past
but breaks in from above. The historical past of
Israel contains no lost paradise, no golden age to
be mourned in nostalgic dreams; but it does
guarantee the present activity of God and, above
all, hope for the future:

Thus says the Lord,
   who opens a way in the sea
   and a path in the mighty waters. . . .
Remember not the events of the past,
   the things of long ago consider not;
See, I am doing something new!
   Now it springs forth, do you not perceive it?
In the desert I make a way,
   in the wasteland, rivers. . . .
   for my chosen people to drink (Isa. 43:16-20).

The transformation of the desert into a flowering garden is a new motif in the parallelism with the former Exodus. It reminds us of God's act of creation (Gen. 2-3). It goes beyond the simple idea of a spatial Exodus to the more radical idea of God as creator of something totally new. Thus it bears witness to the yearning of the Israelite believer for a divine act that will give an even surer ground for his hope: a creative act. Man's salvation and redemption become, in Second Isaiah, a creative redemption of man in his totality, from birth to his immortal destiny, from his vicissitudes in our world of time to his life in eternity when history is over.

LET MY PEOPLE GO!

Let my people go! The God of the Bible makes this cry of the Negro spiritual echo still against the Pharaonic powers at work in every age.

The concrete horizon against which the biblical message of salvation is preached is the Exodus; the biblical model of salvation is a dynamic model of liberation. The basic soteriological affirmation of the Bible, therefore, is: "Be free!" And the freedom in question is the freedom which, as a "capacity for the definitive," can alone open to man and the human community the way to full humanization and to a future that is the issue not of a regressive quest for origins but of a hope of newness. The God of the Bible routs the gods of metaphysical cosmology. The cyclic myth of eternal return is definitively superseded by a vision that is wholly focused on the open spaces of freedom and on the attainment of a future which is not simply a development of possibilities contained in man's past but is, rather, something unforeseeably new. The God of the Exodus creates for the human community the category of power, newness, freedom from limitations. Thanks to him creation and history become open-ended realities. The experiential field in which human history deploys its possibilities becomes broadened beyond all expectations.

The God of man's future, the God of newness and freedom, has broken into human history to free it once again. The Unconditioned has entered into the conditioned in order to rouse man to an exodus into freedom in its fullness; in order to commit the human community to the nomadic existence which his truth and freedom require, while rescuing it from helpless subjection to fate.

The man who accepts the God of the Exodus as his companion on life's way destroys at its root the hazard presented by what Ernst Bloch has called the "melancholy of fulfillment"—that is, the danger that we shall grow old and hesitant, adapting ourselves to things as they are, so that we no longer experience the pain of reality and oppose ourselves to it, but instead become its slave. To heed the voice of the God of the Exodus is to feel the "sharp spur of the future cutting inexorably into the flesh of present reality."

The voice of the God of the Exodus gives surety to the Christian hope of freedom, a hope in whose eyes "the world is full of all kinds of possibilities, namely all the possibilities of the God of hope. It sees reality and mankind in the hand of him whose voice calls into history from its end, saying, 'Behold, I make all things new,' and from hearing this word of promise it acquires the freedom to renew life here and to change the face of the world."[6]

In the Old Testament all this is hope and expectation: hope based on the word of promise, which refers man to the future and orientates human history towards the future. This hope and expectation becomes an eschatological expectation, of which an essential element is the promise of universal salvation: salvation for all peoples and for man in the totality of his being.

At the end of time all mankind will see the light shining on the mountain of Yahweh. In a world-wide centripetal movement all peoples will converge upon that light; in it they will find the total fulfillment of all man's needs and desires (Isa. 2:1-4; Mic. 4:1-5; Isa. 29:6-9; etc.). Only "when the fulness of time comes" will Yahweh affirm his lordship over the world in universal and radical terms (cf. Pss. 46, 48; etc.) and the Spirit be fully poured out on the nations and on the human in its every aspect (cf. Acts 2:14-43).[7] The Old Testament simply heralds the eschatological intervention of this God who saves all mankind and all of man.

2

HE WHO KNOWS
THE SORROWS OF MEN

CHRIST, THE ESCHATOLOGICAL
EVENT

*After speaking at length through the Old
Testament prophets, God decided, in the
fullness of time, to offer eschatological
(that is, radical and definitive) salvation by
sending his Word. Christ manifests the full
salvific will and love of God, and he does so
in the most comprehensive and radical way.
Thus he is the last and most explicit Word
of God to men; he is the eschatological
event.*

To encounter Christ means, for any individual and for any people of whatever time and
place, to encounter the salvation which God
offers "once and for all" (cf. Rom. 6:10; 2 Cor.
2:19-20; etc.) and in a definitive way to all men.
The New Testament gives expression to this
central fact through images and categories taken
from the Old Testament. In Christ the Spirit is
poured out in a full and decisive fashion, not
simply on certain individuals or a particular
people, but on mankind as a whole. Christ is *the*
eschatological fruit of the Spirit. His coming
means "This is the time of fulfillment. The reign

of God is at hand!" (Mark 1:15). With him the reign of God, the concrete assertion of God's saving will for mankind, has already begun in human history. The crowd greeted Jesus, as he entered Jerusalem, with the words: "Blessed is he who comes in the name of the Lord! Blessed is the reign of our father David to come!"(Mark 11:10).

Jesus makes God's salvation a reality: he heralds it, offers it, inaugurates it, and anticipates its full and final realization in his own paschal experience. With his coming the time of fulfillment is here: the beginning of the new age, of the new heavens and the new earth. With his coming God has decided to involve himself in human experience in an irrevocable way. In him "God has accepted the world by a definitive, eschatological act" (Johann Baptist Metz).

Christ inaugurates the reign of God and opens the world's doors to salvation. In the comprehensive event which his life in its totality is (a life given eschatological qualification by his resurrection)—in his incarnation, in his activity (miracles), in his death and resurrection—he shows himself to be God's saving action in the world (Hans Conzelmann). The incarnation is the Son of God's self-emptying into our condition of historicity and temporality; in it he makes his own the very tissue of our creaturely being.

Jesus' activity in working miracles is the

sign that a new page of human history has begun, and its newness is unqualified; for this page is the last page, and what is written on it will be determinative for the salvation of all men. It marks the beginning of the "last times": "Jesus toured all of Galilee. He taught in their synagogues, proclaimed the good news of the kingdom, and cured the people of every disease and illness" (Matt. 4:23). His miracles reveal the "cosmic newness" that accompanies the historical newness; in them Christ frees men from the determinations, limits, and conditions imposed by creaturehood and existence in the cosmos, and manifests the sovereignly free intervention in time of the God of the Bible.

In the person of Jesus we find the signs of eschatological salvation of which the prophets had spoken. At the beginning of his public life Jesus describes himself as follows: "The spirit of the Lord is upon me; therefore he has anointed me. He has sent me to bring glad tidings to the poor, to proclaim liberty to captives, recovery of sight to the blind and release to prisoners, to announce a year of favor from the Lord" (Luke 4:18-19).

Christ's death is the high-point in his becoming a man, and the moment of his most total identification with us. It is the declaration that man is powerless to save himself when left to his own resources. It is the statement of mankind's bankruptcy, as it destroys itself in

37

idle, useless, egoistic activity; of man's inherent incompleteness and his need of a salvation that comes from above. It is the stripping bare of humanity, down to its radical poverty, so that it may be exposed to the power of the Spirit.

The resurrection discloses the eschatological dimension of Christ's existence. For in the resurrection Jesus enters the future of God's kingdom and the future glory of God himself. In it God's ancient promises are fulfilled. In it appears that future in which God is God and man is truly himself (Jürgen Moltmann). Christ is the originator of the kingdom on earth, the beinning of the *eschaton,* or final state of things, and of the newness that is to come. As Son of God and Son of man, and as supreme fulfillment of God's fidelity (Juan Alfaro), Christ has made human existence his own, penetrated it to its ultimate depths where it bears the seal of inexorable death, and made it possible for authentic man to come into existence: man the conqueror of limits and of death.

The risen, glorified Christ, now seated at the Father's right hand, has received all authority in heaven and on earth. He has been entrusted with all the power and saving love of the Father, and can therefore say to those who believe in the newness he represents: "Receive my spirit and pour it out on every creature. Now is the time to tell all men of the decisive fact

that determines all of history: I am with you to
the end of the world" (cf. Matt. 28:19).

CHRIST'S MESSAGE IS WHOLLY AND
ENTIRELY MISSIONARY

*To understand Christ as God's saving action
and to understand the eschatological meaning of his life is to grasp the universal,
missionary bearing of the Christ-event.*

Christ and the world are two terms which
call for each other. Christ and mankind are the
two basic poles of reality. Christ came to save
man, and for that alone.

Christ can be, and in fact has been,
sacralized throughout the centuries. He can be,
and in fact has been, relegated to the sacristy
and to churches that are excessively different
from the houses in which men live. He has been,
and can still be today, dolled up and disguised in
garments that are alien to men's experience. The
candles and incense that have surrounded him in
the past and surround him even now can make
him a stranger and unrecognizable. He has often
been given a language and a voice that are not
his own. Yet despite the uses that have been
made of him, the Christ of the Gospels still

manifests certain personality traits that distinguish him from all others. To grasp this Christ and to realize that he is the Word of salvation *for the world,* are one and the same thing. Christ and God's word of salvation *for the world* are the same thing.

"World," insofar as it is correlative to the kingdom of God, is a messianic and eschatological concept. The ends of the earth and the ends of time are correlative and connected ideas (J. C. Hoekendijk). The world, or man in the totality of his human dimensions, is manifestly the space for the proclamation of the kingdom. Christ did not come to divide the world into believers and nonbelievers. Rather, he became the basically important fact for the world, turning the world into man's world and turning man into God's utopia. The God of the Bible has irrevocably linked the world to himself, in Christ. There are two facts that are basic and certain: Christ with his Gospel, on the one hand, and man on the other. Christ as messenger to the world, and the Gospel which must be offered and preached to the world; Christ (kingdom of God)—mission—world. Everything else is relative to this and to be understood in terms of it; everything else is ordered to this movement and pattern. Mission means the message of Christ to the *man of today* in his concrete totality.

CHRIST, JUDGMENT UPON THE WORLD

The very universality of salvation demands a choice. The fact that Christ has brought salvation to man implies, both in Christ and in whoever wishes to follow him, a choice. This choice is always and solely in favor of man as against whatever threatens his freedom.

This heading may seem to contradict what we have been saying, but it really does not. Christ came to bring salvation to all men and to affirm God's universal salvific will. He also said that he brought judgment and the division of the world into two halves; he said that he came to bring war, not peace; in his programmatic messages (sermon on the mountain: cf. Matt. 5-7; Luke 6:20-38; and Luke 4:18-19, already quoted) he made some very clear statements of the critical significance of his coming. To a series of "beatitudes" he adds a series of "woes" (cf. Luke 6:20-38; he adds even more solemn ones in Matt. 23). He says that the path of salvation is narrow and that few walk it to its end. He sets radical conditions for those who wish to follow him (Matt. 13:34-35; Mark 9:47; Luke 9:17; etc.).

It is his limitless love for man that makes Christ divide the world into halves—or, rather, makes him reduce all the oppressive divisions which man introduces into the world to a single division: the division between those who suffer and those who cause suffering. For he is well aware that the evils men suffer have man himself for their cause. Precisely because Christ is so concerned with the destinies of men—with man's salvation and full humanization, his freedom and dignity—he had to make preferential choices, that is, to take the side of the weak against the strong, the oppressed against the oppressor. His aim was not a simple inversion of power relationships: it was rather to eliminate them by transforming them into relationships of freedom, equality, and love.

The "new heavens and new earth" which he inaugurated by bringing God's kingdom to the world are the new mankind for which he lived and died and rose:

As the new heavens and the new earth
*   which I will make*
Shall endure before me, says the Lord,
*   so shall your race and your name endure* (Isa. 66:22).

Christ is also a judgment upon the world in a much more radical sense. The fact that he came to save man and that saving man meant, above all, saving him from his fellow man (the most dangerous to mankind of all the beasts of prey) implies a basic principle, and he directed his saving message primarily to getting this

42

principle across. "Blest are you poor: the reign of God is yours" (Luke 6:20) is simply an explicitation of the statement: "I have come to save man and all mankind."

The special privilege and precedence given here is certainly not based on belonging to a specific race or culture. It refers to an existential situation of poverty, oppression, and exploitation. In Christ the God of the Exodus and of freedom manifests himself in a definitive way. He wages war upon the forces of oppression, not now in favor of a particular people from a particular stock and cultural world, but in favor of all (individuals or groups, whatever their origin) who are oppressed and in any need and who seek freedom. The human areas that are poorest in every way are the most qualified for receiving the saving Word. They are the ones that have the best right to that word; they are the privileged recipients of the Gospel; they are the ones whom Christ and Paul would unhesitatingly seek out in proclaiming salvation. Even in terms of the individual's personal life, the most intensely felt moments of poverty (in the biblical sense) are the privileged moments for hearing the Word and receiving the Spirit.

A further observation is justified: the social, economic, political, and cultural situation provides a hermeneutical norm for the messenger of the Gospel as he endeavors creatively to interpret and effectively to apply the Word he brings. The specific kind of need or poverty requires a specific choice and "professional" preparation on the part of the one who is offered Christ's salvation and to bring it to bear in a concrete way.[8]

CHRIST, JUDGMENT UPON EVERY RELIGIOUS SOCIETY THAT CALLS ITSELF BY HIS NAME

The subject of judgment is not Christ's mission to the world but the Church if, and insofar as, it does not carry out Christ's mission to the world. For mission is the functional, relative reality of the Church, and it is ceaselessly being criticized and judged by the world and by Christ.

Christ must be freed from all the limitations to which the Christian religious bodies, so heavily organized and institutionalized, subject him. For the Church, as an organized society, does not only bear within it the Word which ceaselessly determines its purpose, and the Spirit who ceaselessly renews it; it also contains a number of elements which are part of its social being and which it may share with all organized religious societies. Moreover, insofar as the Church is not permeated by the newness of life which comes from Christ, that is, insofar as it is not related with every fiber of its being both to Christ and to the world, it is in danger of turning the essentially centrifugal, missionary movement which emanates from Christ and embraces the whole world into a centripetal, propagandistic movement that aims at sectarian proselytizing. Christ's message tends of its nature to transcend the limits of religious institutions. Christ calls men and is an answer to men's needs.[9]

It is not an exaggeration to say that only a rediscovery and a concrete awareness of its own being as the mission of Christ to the world can save today's Church and reinsert it into the movement of human history. Only this can keep it from losing both Christ and the world and from becoming alienated from the definitive, irrevocable dialogue which Christ began with mankind.

And yet even today, in this era of renewal, the symptoms of an unhealthy introversion are observable at every level of the Church's activity. This fact provides an easily applicable criterion for judging the evangelical authenticity of any initiative, program, activity, or new departure that arises in the churches of our experience. Even the ecumenical movement, and the organizations which represent, if not the spirit and evangelical thrust of the movement, at least its program of operation, are in danger of becoming a cooperative movement of defense against the world if they fail to situate themselves within this wholly missionary perspective. Only thus can they represent an authentic quest for and implementation of the values of the Gospel.

A certain sign of evangelical authenticity is the ability of the Church, or of any ecclesial community, to be a startling new fact in the world—like the Christ-event; to have something to say in the world and to the world that is really new. But there is a constant temptation to evade this kind of encounter with the world, this kind of direct judgment by the world. There is a constant temptation, too, to contain Christ's offer of salvation within what is thought of as the religious sphere, whereas in fact it embraces the totality of the human person.

The world compels the Church to be the Church—to be authentic, true, and poor. It forces the Church to abandon every kind of integrism and triumphalism, such as characterized an ecclesiology that arose, as Gualberto Gualerni notes, in the era when Christianity had become the state religion of some European countries.[10]

URGENCY OF THE MISSION?

Christ exists for the world, and his salvation is already present everywhere. But it is

46

*also true that this salvation is made explicit
and fully realized, in a way that serves as
model and hope for the world, in the
ecclesial community. Ekklesia (the community called by God) and mission require
each other.*

Christ is salvation for all mankind. He
accepts it and redeems it from within, in its
entirety. He makes his own the whole life of
man with its need and poverty, and brings it
radical healing. His saving action is, of itself,
directed beyond the limits of the visible Church.
Given that the Son of God became truly man,
man has become the place in which definitive
relationships are established between God, on
the one side, and man and the world, on the
other.[11] In Christ the whole human community
enters into relationship with God. In Christ the
whole world has already become a saved world,
even if saved "in hope,"[12] for it is a hope that
cannot be deceived, inasmuch as it rests upon
God's irrevocable word in Christ and that word
is operative in us and in the world through the
Spirit (cf. Rom. 8:14-38). In the resurrection of
Christ the world was set under the sign of God's
definitive victory, in Christ, over the forces of
destruction.

Once the divinity had manifested itself
clearly and in a fully concrete human way; once
the revelation of the divine had taken place fully

47

and definitively in Jesus, who is the human brought to perfection, the perfect man, the hypostatized ideal, as it were, of human nature, no less than the definitive human Word of God; once the concrete human condition of Jesus had become the place where God reveals himself: —then all that is specifically human became the material of revelation.

> Historical contact with the Church, therefore, is not the most important thing. A man's very attitude towards his fellow human being already involves decisions for or against salvation. . . . Wherever there are men, wherever there is the experience of human existence, there the revelation and grace of God are concretely at work. . . . The saving mystery is already silently present in human life, before the name of that mystery is revealed in the Church of Christ.[13]

But if it is true that the eschatological salvation brought by Christ is in fact already effectively present in all mankind, wherever men exist and in all areas of their lives, then why should there be any urgency to mission?

Mission is urgent, imperative, and incumbent upon us only if, and to the extent that, it aims at rendering explicit—and does in fact effectively make explicit and clear, in the event which is the Church of Christ—that salvation which is already actively present in all of mankind. In this sense, and for this reason, the mission can only take the form of an ecclesial mission, as the ecclesial manifestation, complete and explicit, of the salvation already present in the world.

Only if the mission takes a communal, ecclesial form in the event we call the Church will the Church be authentically Christ's mission. For "it [the Church] reveals the world to itself and does so in such a fashion that the world sees what it itself really is and what it can become by the power of God's gift of grace. The Church, therefore, hopes not only for itself but for that whole world which it serves."[14]

Thus we cannot put off talking about the Church any longer. That will be our subject in the next chapter.

3

MISSION
AND SECULARIZATION

NEED OF THE CHURCH
DESPITE THE CHURCH

We have said that if the Church is to be the Church it must be missionary. The statement can be reversed: if the mission is to be the mission of Christ, it must become an ecclesial mission, a mission of the Church, a mission which brings the Church into existence and is carried out by the Church. The Church needs the mission, and the mission needs the Church.

Would it not be a good thing if, for a while, we stopped talking about the "Church"? The term is too vague and ambiguous, worn-out and heavy with alien resonances. It fails to rouse adverse feelings only in those who realize that "ecclesial" is an English derivative from the Greek word *ekklesia,* and who therefore immediately give the word its biblical and evangelical meaning. According to the latter, *ekklesia* is the eschatological community of salvation; the community which, in faith, encounters the definitive Word of God and is thereby faced with an inescapable choice. The community is the human locus in which the Spirit once again generates the Word; it is the desert in which the Spirit causes manna to drop down and makes water spring forth; it is the "explicit" place where the God of Christ is present to the world; it is the "spiritual" (Spirit-effected) organism, the "spiritual" body, that is, the whole Christ, the place where God's word of salvation becomes transparent to mankind.

The "Church," however, is many things, and some of these are far from pleasing. The sharp eye that would compare Church and Gospel, Church and Christ, cannot fail to note contrasts which give rise to painful reflections.

When taken as an organized religious society and thus from the standpoint of the history of religions, the Church is of course not entirely new. It shares in the double character that the other religions have. A religion can, on the one hand, represent the heights of the spirit and be a liberating agent. On the other hand, no apologetics can gloss over the fact that in its concrete forms religion often has its negative side. Religion has produced not only the loftiest flights of the human spirit but also the most fearful fanaticisms and every kind of human alienation and depravity.[15]

The ambivalence of religion (viewed generally) is recognizable today at every psychological and sociological level. It is no longer possible simply to ignore the charge that religion is an agent of human alienation and humiliation; it often has only too much validity, even with reference to Christianity. A sociological approach to the historical reality of the "Church" is required today if we are to explain many phenomena and if we are not to be nonplussed by many things, past and present, within the Church.

But the socio-politico-cultural context (this is essentially ambiguous, as we noted before) which necessarily shapes the life of the Church should not prevent an ongoing rediscovery within the Church of the new thing which Christ represents in regard to mankind's salvation. Nor should the Church be the constant target and whipping-boy for criticisms related to its historical situation. The psychological energy thus consumed seems really excessive and disproportionate, inasmuch as what are involved are certain obvious facts of social life. The specific element in Christian newness, on the contrary, will never be an ordinary component of social reality, even of ecclesial social reality, but will always be a fruit of the Holy Spirit who comes from on high and works his will in the desert of human poverty. This is why the specific element of faith often expresses itself by way of contrast to what is socially evident and obvious.

Having said all of this as a stimulus to reflection and to a more specific and far-reaching discussion than we can engage in here, we must say without hesitation that the mission is not the affair of single individuals. The mission of Christ to the world is a community, or ecclesial, event. The mission needs the Church.

In the Old Testament God chose individuals as prophets, priests, and kings, and sent his spirit upon them that they might communicate his salvation to the people. The new thing about Christianity is that Christ established a whole people of prophets, priests, and kings, a royal, prophetic, and priestly people (1 Pet. 2:9), and that the Spirit is the new reality in which the *whole* people shares. That people thus becomes, as such, a *mission* of salvation to mankind.

Christ, when preached, establishes the Church. Out of the hearing of the Gospel (which has the Christ-event for its object and content) the Church is born. The Church is truly the Church if, in its turn, it becomes a concrete embodiment of this Gospel in the eyes of the world.

We shall develop two points on this subject:

1) If the Church wants to be authentic, that is, if it wants to be God's mission to the world, as Christ was, it must be wholly and solely shaped by the Spirit: Spirit and Mission (our subject in the remaining pages of the present chapter).

56

2) The Church is mission when it is the concrete embodiment, in historical, human time and space, of the integral offer of salvation which Christ makes to man. It is such an embodiment when it is marked by communion (*koinōnia*), service (*diakonia*), and preaching (*kerygma*). (This will be the subject of the next chapter.)

MOVED BY THE SPIRIT

"The Holy Spirit and mission are the signs of the final phase, in which we live and which is oriented to the future" (Joachim Jeremias). The Spirit makes possible, stimulates, and brings to pass a personal discovery of Christ; he makes it possible for this word of salvation to be spoken to the world, that is, he makes mission possible.

An evident condition for being a Christian (a man sent by Christ to the world, a man born of God and his Spirit, not of flesh and blood; the fruit and offspring of the promise and not of the law; of life and not of genealogies) is the always personal discovery of Christ as God's *eschaton* and as total newness. A personal actualization of the Christian reality is indispensable, for that is the meaning of faith, understood as acceptance of a Person, as adherence to him and complete involvement with him and for him.

To believe means to possess the Spirit of Christ. To believe means to draw upon all one's inner energies, as stirred up and set in movement precisely by the Spirit, in order to give the Christ-event a new incarnation at every moment and to speak that event forth to others.

A personal actualization of the Gospel is a prerequisite of mission. Such a personal actualization is possible, however, only if one has the Spirit of Christ, and thanks to that Spirit.

A personal realization of Christ's message in its communal, ecclesial dimensions is a condition of mission because the Christian community is missionary, that is, it is the offering to the world of that integral salvation won by Christ. But this realization of the Gospel message in community form is in turn possible only where the Spirit of Christ is the center of the individual's action and efforts, which thereby become so many forces fostering the freedom and humanization of our brothers.

The gift of the Spirit is presupposed by mission, as even a brief glance at the New Testament will show us. Let us look at the Spirit-mission relationship in Acts, John, and Paul.

The missionary book beyond all others, the Acts of the Apostles, is a continuous testimony to a single fact: those who receive the Spirit magnify the Lord, that is, they proclaim his marvelous saving acts to others. Four passages in Acts speak of the descent of the Spirit. The first is the one "describing" Pentecost and the beinning of the Church: Acts 2:1-13. The second concludes the narrative of Peter's liberation from prison: Acts 4:31. The third occurs in the story of Cornelius' conversion: Acts 10:44-45. The fourth involves Paul: Acts 19:6.

In the first three of these passages the Spirit's descent upon believers is accompanied by cosmic phenomena (described or simply mentioned), such as had already marked, in the Old Testament, the theophanies or manifestations of God's saving power (cf. Exod. 19; Nah. 1). In the fourth, the Spirit is communicated through the imposition of hands. All four passages on the descent of the Spirit contain three points which are basic for understanding the connection between the Spirit and the Church as mission:

1) The descent of Christ's Spirit as spirit of the first creation and the new creation, messianic and eschatological spirit, final embodiment of God's salvation: Gen. 1; Ezek. 37; 2 Isa. 32:15-20; 44:1-5; Ezek. 11:18-20; Jer. 31; Joel 3:1-5 (this passage is quoted and given a messianic, eschatological interpretation in the first missionary discourse, which the book of Acts puts on the lips of Peter and which shows a

A) Acts 2:1-14	B) Acts 4:31
When the day of Pentecost came, it found them gathered in one place.	*(After the freeing of Peter and as they prayed)*
1a *Suddenly from up in the sky there came a noise like a strong, driving wind. . . .*	*The place where they were gathered shook. . . .*
b *Tongues as of fire appeared, which parted and came to rest on each of them.*	
2 *All were filled with the Holy Spirit.*	*They were filled with the Holy Spirit*
3 *They began to express themselves in foreign tongues and make bold proclamation as the Spirit prompted them.*	
4 *Peter stood up with the Eleven, raised his voice, and addressed them.*	*and continued to speak God's word with confidence.*

pattern and content similar to those of the other great missionary sermons of Acts; cf. 2:14-39; 3:13-26; [4:10-12; 5:30-32]; 10:36-43; 13:17-41 [this speech attributed to Paul] [16]).

2) The gift of tongues (lacking in the second discourse), which is one of the charisms, or gifts, of the early Church: 1 Cor. 12-14.

C) Acts 10:44-45

(After Peter's words, suddenly)

D) Acts 19:6

As Paul laid his hands on them,

the Holy Spirit descended upon all. . . .

They could hear [the Gentiles] speaking in tongues

and glorifying God.

the Holy Spirit came down on them

and they began to speak in tongues

and to utter prophecies.

---

3) Speaking out "with confidence" (Acts 4:31) the word and the *kerygma* (2:4), the great deeds of God (10:44); in other words, the prophetic activity (19:6) which follows "necessarily" and logically from the reception of the Spirit. This is the missionary activity of all who have received the Spirit.

In order to grasp and to proclaim Christ as God's saving, eschatological action a man must receive Christ's Spirit. Inversely, all those who have the Spirit of Christ are automatically constituted, in a basic way, his missionaries, his apostles, delegated and sent forth to communicate that Spirit.

In the Fourth Gospel, too, the gift of the Spirit is linked with the eschatogical Christ-event which reached its fulfillment in his death and resurrection. "There was . . . no Spirit as yet, since Jesus had not yet been glorified" (John 7:39). "If I fail to go, the Paraclete will never come to you, whereas if I go, I will send him to you" (John 16:7; cf. 15:26; 16:13-15, 17).

John sees in the crucifixion the moment of Christ's glorification and the assertion of his universal lordship over creation. "I—once I am lifted up from the earth—will draw all men to myself" (John 12:32). More than that, in this one act are concentrated the three elements which make up the *eschaton* or eschatological saving action which God carries out in Christ: the cross, the glorification, and the outpouring of the Spirit. "When Jesus took the wine, he said, 'Now it is finished.' Then he bowed his head, and delivered over his spirit" (John 19:30).

Elsewhere John clearly connects the outpouring of the Spirit, as fruit of Christ's death and resurrection, with mission. "Then he breathed on them and said: 'Receive the Holy Spirit. If you forgive men's sins, they are forgiven them; if you hold them bound, they are held bound' " (John 20:22-23).

Again, for John, in an even more explicit and anthropological way than for the author of Acts, the Spirit is the one who alone can give understanding of Christ as total newness: "A little while now and the world will see me no more; but you will see me as one who has life, and you will have life. . . . This much have I told you while I was still with you; the Paraclete, the Holy Spirit whom the Father will send in my name, will instruct you in everything, and remind you of all that I told you" (John 14:18, 25-26).

The Spirit is not only necessary if we are to understand, discover, and live Christ in a personal way; he is also necessary if we are to proclaim Christ, to speak him to others. "When the Paraclete comes, the Spirit of truth who comes from the Father—and whom I myself will send from the Father—he will bear witness on my behalf. [He will do so in such a way that you will understand his witness concerning me and discover me as total newness, and *therefore*:] You must bear witness on my behalf, for you have been with me from the beginning" (John 15:26-27).

We should observe how close the relation is between the theologies of Spirit-inspired mission in John and Acts. In Acts the Spirit is the manifestation-understanding of God's great deeds and especially of the climactic deed which is Christ; the immediate result of his coming is the proclamation to mankind of this saving event. The same is true in John: the Spirit is the inner power which enables men to understand Christ; consequently he is the capacity and power to "bear witness to Christ" before others.

In Paul we find the same basic ideas: the Spirit is the power divinely given me of linking myself to the destiny of Christ; he is Christ acting in me; he gives himself to me that he may bestow upon me the utmost in Christian individuality and personality; the latter finds its connatural manifestation when I make of myself a liberating and saving gift for others, when I express and give Christ, who is man's salvation, to my brother in the concrete reality of his life.

The Spirit, for Paul, is the active, creative presence of the risen Christ in the believer, in all who believe. His gifts (charisms)—which really means his self-gift to us in a personal, divine way—are able to assure each believer the maximum of individuality and personality and, consequently, a total availability to others. "We have gifts that differ according to the favor bestowed on each of us. One's gift may be prophecy; its use should be in proportion to his faith. It may be the gift of ministry; it should be used for service. One who is a teacher should use his gift for teaching; one with the power of exhortation should exhort. He who gives alms should do so generously; he who rules should exercise his authority with care; he who performs works of mercy should do so cheerfully" (Rom. 12:6-8).

The Spirit evokes and confirms dedication to Christ and the brethren, and welds believers into a single "spiritual" body. He is the God of Christ in us, closer to us, indeed, than we are to ourselves. He saves us as persons, and molding us from within, makes us more fully human. He saves us and liberates us in our very volition and free choice. His action does not eliminate human initiative, but on the contrary awakens it to greater vigor and authenticity; he does not free us of the burden of decision but makes us able to decide with full Christian freedom.

The Spirit thus is the cause, for the individual Christian and for the ecclesial community, of a more authentic, genuine existence. He is the Christian God: a God within us, and the final revelation of the God who hides himself in his very manifestation, so as to safeguard our freedom; who veils himself in manhood, so as to make man fully human. He is the unnamed and unnamable God who is shrouded in mystery. He defends his freedom against all the false images and manipulations into which men attempt to coerce him; in so doing, he also defends the freedom of man and the hopes of man.

He creates the sphere in which genuine freedom and humanization is possible. He creates the new heavens and new earth, the promised land where God's rule over man leads to man's freedom and authenticity and where each individual, precisely because he is truly himself, is able to communicate all his personal riches to his brother, thus becoming a source of harmony and positive union. Peace, as the sum-total of messianic blessings, is the characteristic effect of the eschatological gift of the Spirit to the community of the saved.

As "spiritual," this community is also, of its nature, missionary. Paul speaks of missionary activity, the apostolate, as "the ministry of the Spirit" (2 Cor. 3:8). The gift of the Spirit is a necessary presupposition if a community is to be an authentically missionary community.

SPIRIT AND MISSION

If all who believe in Christ have the Spirit, all are automatically responsible for Christ's mission to the world. Apostolicity is a basic characteristic note of the Church, that is, of the whole ecclesial community and all its members. "Apostolic succession"

66

*involves everyone, even if in different ways
(according to each one's "gift" and the role
he plays in the community). Apostolic
succession means, in its deepest sense: an
existential accord with the message of
Christ, as authentically transmitted by the
Church of the Apostles, and a concrete
responsiveness to its exigencies.*

We can therefore say, by way of summary, that the Spirit of Christ in us: (1) is a source of personalization and inner dynamism; (2) leads us to an understanding of Christ and guides us to full participation in his life (1 Cor. 1:9; 1 Thess. 4:17; Rom. 8:2; Phil. 3:21); (3) "obliges" us from within to mission: that is, obliges us to speak Christ forth to the world, to proclaim in words and actions the salvation of God (which is summed up in Christ) and his salvific action in the world; (4) inserts into the Christian and the ecclesial community a dynamic principle of continual challenge to reality as it now is, and of nonconformity to it; and rouses and urges Christians to change the pattern of the world; (5) and, as the God of Christ and of the *eschaton,* is unnamed and unnamable, cannot be manipulated, and is totally free.

The Spirit is thus the saving presence of Christ in the world and in all mankind.[17]

With the coming of the Spirit the new creation is already begun; the new heavens and the new earth are already coming into being. Those who possess him have already attained salvation in hope and are on the way to its total achievement. They are the workers who are building on earth the world which is to come.

Some observations on the foregoing summary:

The Spirit is a source of personalization: he does not annihilate individuality in order to make the person simply an example of a category: on the contrary, he further differentiates and perfects capacities and tendencies in line with the person's specific endowment. His influence is never deadening nor leveling: he does not diminish the person of whom he takes possession or do him any violence. He does not drain a man of his humanity or so divinize him that he becomes simply a manifestation of the Spirit; man does not become the equal of a usurper of the divine. The Spirit accepts the other as different from himself and confirms him in his otherness, leaving it whole and intact. He thus restores the person to full and total authenticity: to his own truth and his own freedom. The Spirit calls each to his most fully personal vocation. The Christian who is moved by the Spirit is, beyond all others, the independent and unconditioned man. His autonomous personality enriches society and the world as he lives his life in a fully human and personal way.

The Spirit makes us understand Jesus, the

Christ: that is, the Spirit is the gift from on high who accomplishes his purpose in the poverty, virginity, and sterility of any man who is aware of his impotence and incompleteness, prays and has faith, seeks and receives from on high the answer to his quest and his poverty. The discovery of Christ is a highly personal vital experience. The discovering of Christ (and without that discovery we cannot proclaim him) can never be the professional business of a specific group or social class, made up of "skilled" people who are instructed and put through a course of study for the purpose. Such a training may serve as preparation for professional propagandists, but not missionaries with the Spirit of Christ.

The Spirit "obliges" us from within to mission. The "obligation" arises from within us, not from outside; it is an imperative deriving from an indicative. It is an impulse to be what we are and to act in ways that manifest our insertion into Christ and our being moved by the Spirit, our personal communion with Christ in his Spirit, and therefore our capacity to become creators of freedom, as Christ in his Spirit is.

If the Spirit enables us to know Christ and to proclaim him to others, if he is the basic condition for grasping Christ's message and transmitting it to the world, it follows that *all* those who have the Spirit are able to understand and proclaim Christ. They are, and must be, basically and by their nature missionaries. What is at issue is the completeness of the message and its integrity and effectiveness for all men and for every sphere of human existence: for each person has *his* gift from Christ's Spirit and therefore his own way of presenting Christ's salvation to the world.

Since Christ is sent to save the world, it is necessary that there be a community to carry on this mission: a community with a variety of charisms, ministries, and services, with rich and varied manifestations and activities. If Christ does not mean salvation for man in his totality, for every man, and for every kind of man and society, then there is no eschatological event, no missionary preaching, no universal salvation and renewal, no salt of the earth or light of the world.

To limit and sacralize the mission, that is, to engage in a mission that depends on a religious society or a sacral community, is to denature the community which effects such a limitation.

The Church is wholly and solely apostolic, in the sense that, on the one hand, it is linked to the Church of the Apostles by substantial fidelity to its preaching and doctrine, and, on the other, is totally and in all its members dedicated to the apostolate. Fidelity to the Church's origins really consists in continuing to be basically apostolic, that is, dedicated to universal mission.

It is as a whole that the Church has an apostolic mission and "powers" and is successor to the apostolic Church. The fact that until recently this doctrine was applied only to a clerical class and given juridical formulation has meant the excessive development of certain ministries and functions within the Church.[18] Yet apostolic succession really means succession not only to the apostles but also to the prophets, the teachers, the deacons, and indeed to all the charismatic callings. Only a Church that is fully apostolic and exists fully in the line of apostolic succession can be a Church of Christ, that is, a missionary Church. Only such a Church can be a living missionary proclamation to man in his totality.

MISSION AND SECULARIZATION

On the subsidiary (or less than susidiary!) function of the laity in the Church's mission.

We hear a good deal about laymen and priests; a good deal about the subsidiary role of the laity and the principal role of the priests in missionary activity. Yet if we are going to give Christ to the world we must, obviously, have first understood both Christ and the world; we must be living the Christ-life in the world. But living in the world means sharing in its social, familial, economic, and political problems. So we shouldn't be talking about the laity as playing a subsidiary role relative to priests, but just the opposite. For today it is the laity who can be the authentic expression of Christ's mission to the world.

We need to declericalize our missionary institutes, and to do it from within. We need to restructure them to bring them more into line with lay standards, eliminating class distinctions. (Divisions between brothers and priests are still to be found in these institutes, and the pseudo-problems of harmonizing the two categories—problems which nonetheless require and receive a good deal of attention at chapters and in revised constitutions.) Such a renewal will be possible only if the young members of these institutes become aware of a fundamental datum: missionary activity is not to be identi-fied with priestly activity but requires profes-sional preparation and a professional outlook; that is, the ability to enter into a foreign culture in a well-defined way and to contribute from within to that society's development on the basis of professional qualifications.

If mission, as continuation of Christ's mission to the world, is to be an answer to man's need of salvation in every area and at every level of his life, then missionary activity must be able to play an effective role in all these human spheres. If the various institutes are to claim to be the effective expression today of the missionary thrust of the ecclesial communities, then they must have in their ranks people who are able to act effectively in all areas of human life, whether social or individual. They must have the ability to prepare not only theologians and liturgists but agronomists, doctors, educators, instructors, nurses, etc., as well.

Laymen can exercise a true mission. But they must be genuine laymen, not tame hangers-on of the clergy. They must be laymen who do not need ecclesiastical structures to help them be themselves and to walk the roads of life, men who have discovered Christ as meaning constant risk and involvement. They must be men who aim to bring Christ to other men; men who indeed have respect for rights of precedence, but as these have been determined by Christ, for whom "the least of my brothers" come first. This preference determines very precise norms of action at all levels: in the ecclesial communities of their own country, as they confront the various areas of human life which form their social context; in the local communities as they confront the "mission lands" which still exist in our world; etc. Wherever the soliciting love of Christ is proclaimed with full vigor, there Paul's cry takes on its perennial yet ever relevant meaning: Woe is me if I do not preach the Gospel!

4

CHRISTIANS IN
MISSIONARY COMMUNITIES

MISSIONARY COMMUNITIES

The Christian personality, which is promised a man by the indwelling Spirit, is authentically tested and grows through relationships with his brothers, through dedicated service to man's salvation, and through the positive and explicit proclamation of the Gospel.

Christ's offer of salvation does not take the form of a code of laws but of a concrete model of life together, a model which, therefore, cannot be imitated in solitude. The Spirit who aids the individual Christian personality in its development is, beyond all else, a gift, and therefore makes of each Christian in his turn a liberating gift to his brother.

Christ's salvation becomes a reality in a concrete human group, a human community. What, concretely, are the distinctive characteristics of such a group? The authenticity of their faith in Christ and their Christian existence will, after all, be the concrete measure of the extent to which they carry on Christ's mission to the world.

How can we specify these ideas?

To begin with, let us recall one of our basic guiding principles. The salvation Christ brings is missionary in a universal way, and this in two senses: this salvation is meant for all men of all times and races; and it is meant for man in the totality of his concerns and areas of life and activity—personal, familial, social, political, etc. A Christian community is therefore truly a salvific mission of Christ to men when it is potentially directed to man in his totality and to all men.

Some of the great missiologists have endeavored to pinpoint the basic characteristics of a Christian community which is authentically Christian and therefore missionary.

J. C. Hoekendijk (Dutch missiologist) and his school, for example, claim that where the community does not render an authentic service (*diakonia*) to the world in which it lives, as well as a genuine witness of internal communion (*koinōnia*), the community's mission lacks identity and meaning. For this school the preaching of the Gospel (*kerygma*) is, of course, also essential, but the preaching is understood as taking the form primarily of a concrete witness through action and word.

For another important missiologist, Leslie Newbigin, communion (*koinōnia*) within the Christian community is the indispensable basis upon which witness (*martyria*) and service (*diakonia*) are built.

It seems, then, without making any effort towards an exhaustive study, that we can group the basic characteristics of a missionary community around the three themes of communion (*koinōnia*), service (*diakonia*), and preaching (*kerygma*); these three are also basic in the Bible. The Christian community is its true self, and therefore transcends itself in order to be a saving word to contemporary man and his world, when these three elements are present: communion within the community, service to the whole human community within which the ecclesial community lives, positive and explicit preaching of the Gospel message to the world.

If we wish to speak of the more salient traits of the early communities depicted in Scripture, these three elements will perhaps prove to be focal, even if the accents are differently put in the different communities. Let us look briefly at the three most important local communities in the early Church: Jerusalem, Antioch, and Corinth.

THE CHURCH CEASES TO BE AN ABSTRACTION: THE LOCAL COMMUNITIES IN THE NEW TESTAMENT

Jerusalem, Antioch, and Corinth were three quite different communities: sociologically, ethnically, culturally, and religiously. They were also basically missionary communities.

Our knowledge of the Jerusalem community comes primarily from Acts 1-15. In this community, as far as the Lukan account enables us to judge (for the account is a good deal later

---

Acts 2:41-47

Those who accepted his message were baptized; some three thousand were added that day.

a) *They devoted themselves to the apostles' instruction and the communal life, to the breaking of bread and the prayers.*

b) *A reverent fear overtook them all, for many wonders and signs were performed by the apostles.*

c) *Those who believed shared all things in common; they would sell their property and goods, dividing everything on the basis of each one's need.*

a) *They went to the temple area together every day, while in their homes they broke bread. With exultant and sincere hearts they took their meals in common, praising God and winning the approval of all the people.*

d) *Day by day the Lord added to their number those who were being saved.*

Acts 4:32-35

c) *The community of believers were of one heart and one mind. None of them ever claimed anything as his own; rather, everything was held in common.*

b) *With power the apostles bore witness to the*

than the events and is shaped by theological rather than historical requirements), priority was given to the element of brotherly communion as expressed in devotion to the instruction of the apostles, participation in common prayer and the breaking of bread, and the sharing of material possessions. We find reference to all this

---

resurrection of the Lord Jesus, and great respect was paid to them all;

c) nor was there anyone needy among them, for all who owned property or houses sold them and donated the proceeds. They used to lay them at the feet of the apostles to be distributed to everyone according to his need.

Acts 5:11-16

b) Great fear came on the whole church and on all who heard of it. Through the hands of the apostles, many signs and wonders occurred among the people.

a) By mutual agreement they used to meet in Solomon's Portico. No one else dared to join them, despite the fact that the people held them in high esteem.

d) Nevertheless more and more believers, men and women in great numbers, were continually added to the Lord.

b) The people carried the sick into the streets and laid them on cots and mattresses, so that when Peter passed by at least his shadow might fall on one or another of them. Crowds from the towns around Jerusalem would gather, too, bringing their sick and those who were troubled with unclean spirits, all of whom were cured.

81

in Acts 2:41-47; 4:32-35; 5:11-16, which are editorial summaries intended to highlight typical aspects of Jerusalem, the mother community. These characteristics are: (1) unity centered on the Eucharist and the apostles; (2) active and evident presence of eschatological salvation in the community; (3) community of possessions and hearts; (4) missionary growth of the community.

Jerusalem was the first Christian community, made up for the most part of local Jewish converts, but also containing converts from the Diaspora and from paganism (the "Hellenists": Acts 6:1). It was therefore a pluralistic community, racially and socially as well as culturally and religiously.

Its life-style was somewhat legalistic. That life, as described by Luke around 80 A.D. (and his purpose, let us remember, was not simply to write a historical narrative), was centered upon the Twelve, as witnesses of Jesus' resurrection, with Peter at their head. The apostolic group must soon have been complemented (along the lines of the Jewish synodal community) by a group of elders or "presbyters" who constituted a conservative force in the development of the community and in the community's interaction with the community of Antioch. These elders did not have a specifically cultic role. On the contrary, they must have been administrative people, probably former Pharisees, who shared with the Twelve the responsibility of governing the community. Among them James, brother of the Lord, came to the fore, and would within limits have immediate responsibility for the community, once Peter had left Jerusalem for good (Acts 12:17). The fact that he belonged to the family of Jesus may have influenced the choice of James for this position. In fact, a dynastic mentality seems to have determined the choice of the heads of the Jerusalem community. For after James came Simon, who was replaced in turn by the son of Jude, the third "brother of the Lord."

The Judaizing, conservative hierarchy which ruled the Jerusalem community caused deep tensions in the early communities. They did so by their claim that Christians of pagan extraction must accept the observance of the Mosaic law, especially of its ritual. It would be Paul's task to proclaim with great vigor the definitive break between Christianity and the Jewish synagogue, and indeed between Christianity and every form of sectarian, proselytizing religion. But even before Paul, Peter had an experience which was decisive for the missionary orientation of the Jerusalem Church. He was led to take the initiative in preaching the Gospel and baptizing Cornelius, the centurion (Acts 10). The reaction of Peter's fellow-Christians at Jerusalem was amazement, for they did not understand how the Spirit could descend on pagans too.

This attitude on the part of the Jerusalem community generated opposition to mission, and the community openly accused Peter on his return from Caesarea: "You entered the house of uncircumcised men and ate with them" (Acts 11:2). The result was tension that grew until it was resolved by the Council of Jerusalem (Acts 15), at which Peter affirmed the radical freedom of the Christian and the universality of salvation. James proposed, by way of practical solution, a compromise formula which would secure the peaceful coexistence of Jews and Gentiles within the Church, and the Council accepted the formula (Acts 15:19-22).

Despite his indecision and inconsistency in action (cf. Gal. 2:11-14), Peter was the one who roused and fostered the missionary spirit in the Jerusalem community, until he finally left it (Acts 12:17) in order to be present in person in the Gentile communities.

Conservative tendencies and the problems generated by its links with Jewish tradition, the temptation of introversion and self-sufficiency, ethical rigorism and religious exclusivity, characterized this first community. Yet it was an authentically Christian community, one that found salvation thanks to its undeniable dimensions of internal communion, service (cf. its deacons: Acts 6), and the positive, missionary preaching of the Gospel to the pagans.

The Antioch community provides perhaps

the best model of a missionary community. It was established by Christians from Cyprus and Cyrene and was characterized from the very beginning by a spontaneous openness to Gentiles (Acts 11:20-21).

Here Christ's disciples were called Christians for the first time. The fact is evidence of a clear awareness by the community of its own personality and originality. Barnabas seems to have been the leading man of the community. He had been born in the Diaspora (Acts 4:35) and had lived at Jerusalem as one of the first members of that Christian community; it sent him to Antioch to examine the good dispositions of the many pagan converts, of whom notice had been sent to Jerusalem. Barnabas found the community congenial, and he decided to stay there with Paul (Acts 11:23-26). They did not live there, however, as heads of a cultural or administrative structure of the local Church (wholly dissociated from the synagogue, the Church probably structured itself from the beginning in the form of small domestic communities within which the "prophets" and "teachers" exercised their ministry; cf. Acts 11:27). Instead, Barnabas and Paul were missionaries, sent by the community to preach the Gospel. Thus they gave a needed and imposing expression to the community's authentically Christian character. "On one occasion, while they were engaged in the liturgy of the Lord and were fasting, the Holy Spirit spoke to them: 'Set apart Barnabas and Saul for me to do the work for which I have called them.' Then, after they had fasted and prayed, they imposed hands on them and sent them off" (Acts 13:2-3).

The concern of the Antioch community for the preaching of the Gospel is striking in its spontaneity and in the fact that all the faithful feel a responsibility in this matter. Here, unlike the Jerusalem community, any ministerial arrangement seems to be in function of the preaching of the word rather than of the government of the faithful. Priority goes to the apostle who, in the Lord's name, gathers the assembly of the "called" and converted; then come the prophets, who interpret God's word at community gatherings; then the teachers, who catechize the faithful (Acts 13:1). This community, too, probably had a group of "elders" or "presbyters," but they would have been chosen not by the community but directly by Paul and Barnabas (Acts 14:23).

The preaching of the word and the whole missionary thrust express the ecclesial dynamism which existed in the community. But, in addition to *kerygma,* the element of *diakonia,* or caritative brotherly service, was not lacking. While Jerusalem experienced problems in achieving an equitable distribution of goods within the community (Acts 6), Antioch was sending financial help to all the brethren in Judea (Acts

11:28-30), a gesture which was, above all, the expression of its universalist awareness and its spirit of communion with all the local churches. Paul will invite the Christians of his communities to act in the same way, and he will surely have Antioch's example in mind: 2 Cor. 9:13; Rom. 15:26-27; 2 Cor. 8:14.

The missionary style of the Antioch community and its characteristic universality found vigorous expression in worship as well. According to the *Didache* (10:5), at the end of the breaking of bread, which preceded the Eucharist proper, the celebrant prayed: "Remember your whole Church, Lord, free it from every evil and make it perfect in your love. Gather your sanctified Church from the four winds into the kingdom you have prepared for it."

The Antioch community was one of the most important centers of early Christianity. It was there that the name "Catholic Church" originated, the coinage of its bishop, Ignatius, who was martyred at Rome in the first decade of the second century. And it was in the atmosphere of Antioch that there came to maturity that universalist openness, that missionary expansiveness, and that awareness of catholicity and of communion between all the churches, which were to be the most characteristic notes of every local community.

The community of Corinth. A literary document of the New Testament enables us to

draw the veil aside from the life, tensions, problems, and flowering of one of the most interesting communities in the early Church. The document, of course, is Paul's First Letter to the Corinthians.

During his second missionary journey the apostle had stayed at Corinth for about eighteen months (Acts 18), laboring among the Corinthians with his own hands and preaching the Gospel to the poorest classes in this cosmopolitan city (1 Cor. 1-2). The community was characterized by the variety of people who composed it, and by the abundance and diversity of the charisms which it displayed. In a letter to these Christians—which forms a treatise, even if an unsystematic one, of ecclesiology— Paul lists the sources of division within the community: "fleshly" wisdom, egoism, etc., as well as the sources of communion for any Christian community: the presence of the Spirit in each member of Christ's body, giving everyone the ability to live for others and to be creative instruments of harmony and peace.

The First Letter to the Corinthians contains the most pregnant of all theological expressions for the community-character, the communion, and the unity proper to a local church. The members of a local community, Paul says, are the "Body of Christ." Because of that full solidarity with Christ which possession of the Spirit brings (a solidarity expressed throughout the letter in such phrases as "servants of Christ," "belonging to Christ," "in Christ," "in communion with Christ," "insertion into Christ") and because of his communion with the dead and risen Christ (1 Cor. 15:22-23, 45-47), each Christian is inseparably united to the Lord and becomes "one spirit" with him, that is, member of a single "spiritual" body. The principle of unity in this body is the Spirit, the very Love which unites Father to Son within the Trinity. "Whoever is joined to the Lord becomes one spirit with him" (1 Cor. 6:17).

Such, then, are the patterns of community with which the New Testament provides us. The patterns continue to be programmatic, symbolic, and obligatory for any community that would call itself "apostolic," that is, would claim to be in harmony with the basic idea of the early Church, the Church of the Apostles, as preserved for us in the New Testament writings. When taken together, these models manifest the characteristic traits of communion, service, and missionary preaching.

This brief look at some of the Christian communities in the early Church allows us to draw a conclusion. Only a Christian community which manifests communion (*koinōnia*) between its own members, some kind of authentic service (*diakonia*) that is fully inserted into the social, economic, political, and cultural context, and a preaching (*kerygma*) that is positive, clear, and carried out by all available means, can be called a truly Christian community. Only such a community carries on Christ's mission to man and brings renewal to the world.

Let us briefly consider the three characteristic traits.

KOINŌNIA

In the obedience of all to all there is manifested the Spirit which the risen Christ has communicated to mankind; a local community is the meaningful presence of an ever more perfect communion of all men with each other and with the God of Christ.

We have already noted that the discovery of Christ, always a personal matter, is required by the Gospel message itself. To believe, that is, to have the Spirit, means that the Spirit rouses and sets in motion all of a man's inner energies so that he may at every moment embody in his life the message of Christ. Implementation of the Gospel in one's personal life is a condition of genuine mission. Personal realization of Christ's message within the community is a condition of the community's being truly missionary, that is, of its being a communication of the salvation which God has offered and continues to offer to the world.

Brotherly communion and self-giving to others are the first missionary words which a community speaks to the world. They are the manifestation of that miracle which the Spirit continues to work today as he unites those who believe in Christ and makes of them a "spiritual" body (1 Cor. 6:17).

The fruit and sign of the Spirit's active presence in a community is precisely this obedience of all to all, the mutual love that creates freedom and happiness for others. In this sense, which is fundamental, the Christian community is a "miracle," a "wonderful deed" effected by power from on high; it causes amazement, shocks the onlooker and makes him think, challenges him and forces him to reflect.

Paul develops these ideas primarily in 1 Cor. 2-4 and Rom. 12:8-16: the gift of the Spirit causes each person to be fully himself and to communicate all his personal riches to others; thus the person becomes an agent of that harmony and positive union which are the fruit of the activity and creative sharing by all. In this context the development of professional competences and the preparation for them become a response to the gift of that Spirit who makes us the artisans of freedom and humanization. It is to be noted that peace, as the sum-total of

Messianic blessings, is the characteristic effect of the Spirit, the eschatological Gift.

St. John highlights with special clarity the basic element in Christian newness: "This is how all will know you for my disciples: your love for one another" (John 13:35).

In his First Letter, John describes in three stages the criteria for judging the credibility and authenticity of a Christian community. It is defined first of all as being a community of those who "know" Jesus Christ, that is, who have discovered the newness in him, understood and discerned his true nature, and "have heard . . . seen with our eyes . . . looked upon and our hands have touched" (1 John 1:1).

Well then, says John:

> The way we can be sure of our knowledge of him is to keep his commandments. The man who claims, "I have known him," without keeping his commandments is a liar; in such a one there is no truth. But whoever keeps his word, truly has the love of God been made perfect in him. The way we can be sure we are in union with him is for the man who claims to abide in him to conduct himself just as he did. Dearly beloved, it is no new commandment that I write to you, but an old one which you had from the start. The commandment, now old, is the word you have already heard. On second thought, the commandment that I write you is new, as it is realized in him and you, for the darkness is over and the real light begins to shine. The man who claims to be in light, hating his

brother the while, is in darkness even now. The man who continues in the light is the one who loves his brother; there is nothing in him to cause a fall. But the man who hates his brother is in darkness. He walks in shadows, not knowing where he is going, since the darkness has blinded his eyes (1 John 2:3-11).

In a second stage, the Christian community is defined in terms of sonship. He who believes in Christ is born not of flesh and blood (i.e., not from the striving of human mind or will) but of God (cf. Prologue to Fourth Gospel). Therefore:

No one begotten of God acts sinfully, because he remains of God's stock; he cannot sin because he is begotten of God. That is the way to see who are God's children, and who are the devil's. No one whose actions are unholy belongs to God, nor anyone who fails to love his brother. This, remember, is the message you heard from the beginning: we should love one another. We should not follow the example of Cain who belonged to the evil one and killed his brother. Why did he kill him? Because his own deeds were wicked while his brother's were just. No need, then, brothers, to be surprised if the world hates you. That we have passed from death to life we know because we love the brothers. The man who does not love is among the living dead. Anyone who hates his brother is a murderer, and you know that eternal life abides in no murderer's heart. The way we came to under-stand love was that he laid down his life for us; we too must lay down our lives for our brothers. I ask you, how can God's love survive in a man who has enough of this world's goods yet closes his heart to his brother when he sees him in need? Little children, let us love in deed and in truth and not merely talk about it. This is our way of knowing we are committed to the truth and are at peace before him no matter what our consciences may charge us with; for God is greater than our hearts and all is known to him. Beloved, if our consciences have nothing to charge us with, we can be sure that God is with us and that we will receive at his hands whatever we ask. Why? Because we are keeping his commandments and doing what is pleasing in his sight. His commandment is this: we are to believe in the name of his Son, Jesus Christ, and are to love one another as he commanded us. Those who keep his commandments remain in him and he in them. And this is how we know that he remains in us: from the Spirit that he gave us (1 John 3:9-24).

The flow of thought is elliptical. It picks up the same motif a third time and emphasizes it even more forcefully. Here the discourse reaches its climax. John is speaking of discerning the true fruits of God's Spirit, that is, of distinguishing authentically Christian communities from other religious communities which, apart from the name and some externals, have nothing of the Christian newness in them but simply follow a socio-religious pattern.

Beloved, do not trust every spirit, but put the spirits to a test to see if they belong to God, because many false prophets have appeared in the world. This is how you can recognize God's Spirit: every spirit that acknowledges Jesus Christ come in the flesh belongs to God, while every spirit that fails to acknowledge him does not belong to God. Such is the spirit of the antichrist which, as you have heard, is to come; in fact, it is in the world already. You are of God, you little ones, and thus you have conquered the false prophets. For there is One greater in you than there is in the world. Those others belong to the world; that is why theirs is the language of the world and why the world listens to them. We belong to God and anyone who has knowledge of God gives us a hearing, while anyone who is not of God refuses to hear us. Thus do we distinguish the spirit of truth from the spirit of deception.

Beloved, let us love one another because love is of God; everyone who loves is begotten of God and has knowledge of God. The man without love has known nothing of God, for God is love. God's love was revealed in our midst in this way: he sent his only Son to the world that we might have life through him. Love, then, consists in this: not that we have loved God, but that he has loved us and has sent his Son as an offering for our sins. Beloved, if God has loved us so, we must have the same love for one another. No one has ever seen God. Yet if we love one another God dwells in us, and his love is brought to perfection in us. The way we know we remain in him and he in us is that he has given us of his Spirit. We have seen for ourselves, and can testify, that the Father has sent the Son as savior of the world. When anyone acknowledges that Jesus is the Son of God, God dwells in him and he in God. We have come to know and to believe in the love God has for us. God is love, and he who abides in love abides in God, and God in him. Our love is brought to perfection in this, that we should have confidence on the day of judgment; for our relation to the world is just like his. Love has no room for fear; rather, perfect love casts out all fear. And since fear has to do with punishment, love is not yet perfect in one who is afraid. We, for our part, love because he first loved us. If anyone says, "My love is fixed on God," yet hates his brother, he is a liar. One who has no love for the brother he has seen cannot love the God he has not seen. The commandment we have from him is this: whoever loves God must also love his brother (1 John 4).

The unitive principle which characterizes the missionary community is the Spirit of the final age, whom the risen Christ has merited for us. The fruit and sign of his presence is the peace-unity-solidarity-happiness which is an anticipation of the total peace of eschatological fulfillment.

In this sense we can apply to the local community what Edward Schillebeeckx says of the Church: "In this world the Church is the expressive visibility or meaning-filled presence of a communion of men (already a reality or in process of realization through conversion) in and through their communion with God in Christ.

As thus envisaged it has value in and for itself, but in intrinsic relationship to its mission in the world."[19]

DIAKONIA

The Greek term which the New Testament chooses to apply to a further characteristic of the Christian community is not open to interpretation as implying any position of dignity or authority. Unlike the terms signifying political or ecclesiastical offices, diakonia *refers only to the activity of one who puts himself at the service of another.*

Service—*diakonia*—for Jesus' sake is the characteristic pure and simple of his disciple, and hence of the community which claims fidelity to Jesus. In the New Testament the term retains the disparaging connotations it has in ordinary Greek, for it describes the acts a slave performs for his master when the latter returns home (Luke 17:8); they are services which would not be rendered by a person standing on his dignity. As used by Christ with reference to his disciples, it brings home to us the new and disconcerting nature of his requirements: "Let the greater among you be as the junior, the leader as the servant. Who, in fact, is the

97

greater—he who reclines at table or he who serves the meal? Is it not the one who reclines at table? Yet I am in your midst as the one who serves you" (Luke 22:26-27).

If the local community really wishes to be "the historically permanent existence of Christ," his concrete manifestation "within history that has now become eschatological," then it must prove the legitimacy of its claim by living for others. "The Church does not exist for itself, but for God, for its Lord, for men, and for men's future."[20] This being-for-others is the content of the service which Christ requires (Mark 9:35; 10:43-45; Matt. 20:26-28).

We may apply to the local community and to the Church as a whole the following passage:

The scribes and the Pharisees have succeeded Moses as teachers; therefore, do everything and observe everything they tell you. But do not follow their example. Their words are bold but their deeds are few. They bind up heavy loads, hard to carry, to lay on other men's shoulders, while they themselves will not lift a finger to budge them. All their works are performed to be seen. They widen their phylacteries and wear huge tassels. They are fond of places of honor at banquets and the front seats in synagogues, of marks of respect in public and of being called "Rabbi." As to you, avoid the title "Rabbi." One among you is your teacher, the rest are learners. Do not call anyone on earth your father. Only one is your father, the One in heaven. Avoid being called teachers. Only one is your teacher, the Messiah. The greatest among you will be the one who serves the rest. Whoever exalts himself shall be humbled, but whoever humbles himself shall be exalted (Matt. 23:2-12).

We can also apply to the Church what St. John says: "The man who loves his life loses it, while the man who hates his life in this world preserves it to life eternal. If anyone would serve me, let him follow me; where I am, there will my servant be. If anyone serves me, him the Father will honor" (John 12:25-26).

Therefore, too, what St. John says at a later point must also apply:

After he had washed their feet, he put his cloak back on and reclined at table once more. He said to them: "Do you understand what I just did for you? You address me as 'Teacher' and 'Lord,' and fittingly enough, for that is what I am. But if I washed your feet—I who am Teacher and Lord— then you must wash each other's feet. What I just did was to give you an example: as I have done, so you must do. I solemnly assure you, no slave is greater than his master; no messenger outranks the one who sent him. Once you know all these things, blest will you be if you put them into practice" (John 13:12-17).

The Christian community in its turn acts as a Christian community in accordance with the principle which regulates the life of the individual member. Having attained the highest degree of self-identity and personalization, of specific perfection as a Christian community— that is, a community of men who believe in Christ and are gathered, united, and held together *solely* because they accept him in their lives—it is capable of the maximum of socialization. In other words, the Church is able to integrate itself fully with the world, serving it in all areas, without any loss of autonomy or specific identity.

Above all else, the community's service to the world consists in its capacity for involvement, always and everywhere, on the side of the weak against the strong. But there is always the danger that it will take on the coloration of its environment; and then we hear it said that the Church is like a weathervane, with an infallible sense of which way the wind is blowing: in the play of political, social, and economic forces it will always, at just the right moment, join the winning party. Christ's own strategy was the direct opposite, and that is what he demands of us: a complete independence of all human powers—the poverty and powerlessness which are the conditions of the breakthrough of the Spirit—that places us continuously and totally at the service of the poor.

Service is often the ordeal by fire which tests the missionary spirit and thus the authentically Christian character of a community. The

58516

duty to change the fashion of this world
demands, simultaneously, "nonconformity to
the world" (that is, the preservation and continual reaffirmation of the newness Christ brings)
and complete insertion into it. The Christian
stands for the newness of Christ, for the
beginning of the new heavens and new earth
here in our world. The eschatological hope with
which the Spirit has filled him forces him
continually to challenge reality as it now is. In
this respect the Church is now more than ever
called to prove its true nature by living for
others. In this respect it is undergoing a crisis of
identity. Christian innovation should in truth
give scandal in precisely the way Christ did.
When we cannot tell what a Christian community is really about, or what new thing it has to
say to the rest of the world, we have reason to
doubt its authentically Christian character. If it
is not good for bringing Christ to the world, it is
good for nothing.

The Christian community, which is en-
souled by the Spirit of Christ and saved by and
in Christ, even if only in hope, cannot fail to be
a leaven of renewal in the world:

> A faith which is guided by such a hope is primarily
> not a doctrine, but an initiative for the passionate
> innovating and changing of the world toward the
> Kingdom of God. . . . The future which the
> Church hopes for is not yet here, but is *emerging*
> and *arising* (*entstehend*). Therefore the hope

101

which the Church sets in itself and in the world should be creative and militant. In other words, Christian hope should realize itself in a *creative* and *militant eschatology*. Our eschatological expectation does not look for the heavenly-earthly Jerusalem as that ready-made and existing, promised city of God. This heavenly city does not lie ahead of us as a distant and hidden goal, which needs only to be revealed. The eschatological City of God is *now* coming into existence, for our hopeful approach *builds* this city. We are workers building this future, and not just interpreters of this future.[21]

KERYGMA

The variety of charisms in the Church is limitless, and, since charism and diakonia are correlative, so is the variety of services limitless. Among these services, those of the prophets, teachers, and evangelists stand out, that is, the community functions which deal with a specifically and directly Christian preaching.

The Spirit who is present in each member of the Christian community makes it a community at the service of Christ's mission to the world. "To each person the manifestation of the Spirit is given for the common good" (1 Cor.

12:7). "Put your gifts at the service of one another, each in the measure he has received" (1 Pet. 4:10).

Among these various charisms, however, which are to be found in the New Testament communities, some are more occasional in character or at least are less "official," not always involving the community as such. Others, on the contrary, are communal, public functions. Usually these are also permanent, that is, are given to someone in a regular and continuous way. The New Testament distinguishes even verbally between these two kinds of function within the ecclesial community. For the first (occasional) kind of service it uses the word "gifts," while for the second it designates the persons possessing the charisms by a specific term. In other words, certain functions are connected, in a necessary way and with a certain continuity, to specific persons who are "established" in the Church as apostles, teachers, evangelists, deacons, overseers (*episcopoi*), elders, presbyters (Eph. 4:11; Rom. 12:8-16; etc.).

These permanent services are not always very clearly distinguished from the others. In addition, the dividing line between the various permanent community functions is not always clearly drawn; the prophet, for example, may at the same time be a teacher (that is, a catechist).

But we are interested here only in one

point: among all the charisms and services, those concerned with preaching or the proclamation of the Word take first rank in the New Testament.

The apostles, of course, as foundation and pillars of the Church, take first place; their position too, be it noted, is always described as a ministry and service (Rom. 11:13; 2 Cor. 3:3; 4:1; 6:3-4; 11:8-23; Acts 1:17-25; 20:24; 1 Tim. 1:12). But immediately after them Paul lists two other groups: the prophets and the teachers ("second prophets, third teachers": 1 Cor. 12:28). Their activity consists in the preaching of the word. Such preaching is derived from the foundational witness of the apostles, given once and for all, and must be in harmony with it (Rom. 12:6).

Fidelity to the apostolic witness involves objectivity and courage; it resists the temptation to play down the newness of the Gospel and to conceal the mystery; to avoid the scandal of the Gospel; to be abashed by the perplexity or even ridicule which this absurd message may evoke in its hearers.

At the same time, such fidelity does not mean immobility or rigidity. The preaching of the definitive offer of salvation which God makes in Christ is something quite other than a stereotyped listing of the canons and norms of orthodoxy. Fidelity requires unwearying attention to the real situation the world is in, for this attention will give rise to a creative interpretation and continual concrete application of the message. The constant discovery of the new message which the Gospel brings to any human situation and any human group prevents the *kerygma* from becoming a catechism of formulas presented in the same way in Japan and in the Congo. It obliges the preacher of the word to fidelity not only to his message but also to the cultural world in which the message is to be incarnated.

Study of the Bible, along with the study of sociology, ethnology, and anthropology, may be considered among the most valuable of charisms for the contemporary Church.

PERSONAL VOCATION

The Christian's personal vocation is to be seen within the framework of the community's life; it unfolds as an element, service, and function of the Church's mission as a community.

The vocation of the Christian means, first of all, his being called into the *ekklesia* (community of the called) in order to be a member of it and, as a member, to share in Christ's mission to the world. Christ's offer of salvation cannot be made in a purely individualistic way and by private citizens, as it were. It is, rather, a program of life that can be presented in a concrete, visible way only in a community; the individual's role is to contribute his whole personal wealth to the realization of the program.

How can I contribute to the building up (the biblical, Pauline "edification") of the local community so as to make it the place where the word of God gives its light and Christ continues to reveal and communicate himself within man's history? Where there is no ecclesial event, no concrete actuation of the community in service and preaching, there can be no mission. The reverse is also true: if there is no mission, no clear and inspiring word that leads men to their full human stature and saves them, there can be no true Church.

We have, then, an indication of where we are to start when we wish to inquire into our personal calling. We should not start with our "secondary" vocation to one or other way of life (adherence to this or that organized religious group with its specific orientation within the Church; this or that geographic locale as the scene of our activity). We should start rather with our personal relationship to the *ekklesia*: to communion, service, and proclamation. To be genuinely a Christian, I must launch out in that direction, answering the solicitation of the Spirit to achieve maximal personal fulfillment in relation to Christ whom I receive and communicate to others as the highest achievement of manhood. Given this radical choice as my framework, I will then reflect on the concrete, historical, immediate *way* in which I commit myself, on the *group* in which I shall give my conversion its specific embodiment, and on the *place* where I shall seek to live out the communal dimensions of my life and activity.

It is undeniable that there are various charisms and offices in the Church and that all are "services" rendered to the community so that the community may be a "service" to the world. "There are different gifts but the same Spirit; there are different ministries but the same Lord; there are different works but the same God who accomplishes all of them in everyone. To each person the manifestation of the Spirit is given for the common good" (1 Cor. 12:4-6). In this passage Paul is stressing the point that the variety of charisms and ecclesial ministries is not opposed to the unity of the Church's mission. This is so because the individual function in the Church cannot be made the ground of special privilege but is intended rather to foster the communal sharing of God's people in service; and because the articulation of various functions increases unity by giving involvement with the world a more organic form.

Looking more directly to mission, we can

say that it can be carried out by the Christian community by way either of *diffusion* or of *sending.* Consider the Antioch community (Acts 11:19-26; 13:2-5). On the one hand, we have the Christian community establishing itself by going out to the pagans living there and preaching "the Lord Jesus to them." "The hand of the Lord was with them" (Acts 11:21) as they bore witness to and preached their own faith. Barnabas and Paul joined them and "for a whole year they met with the church and instructed great numbers. It was in Antioch that the disciples were called Christians for the first time" (verse 26). The missionary task was here being carried out in a very vital form by way of "diffusion"; all Christians shared in the task, even if the activity of Barnabas and Paul stimulated, guided, and complemented the communal action.

At a given moment, however, during a liturgical service, the community found itself addressed by the Spirit: "Set apart Barnabas and Saul for me to do the work for which I have called them." This was a *special* mission, distinct from that in which the whole community was involved; for such a special mission, which we are calling a *sending,* some persons were *set apart* by the Spirit, by means of and within the community. "Then, after they had fasted and prayed, they imposed hands on them and sent them off" (Acts 13:2-3). The community cannot resist the choice made by the Spirit, but neither is it uninvolved in that choice. It accepts and ratifies what the Spirit shows that he wants.

Every time mission becomes a fully vital reality in a Christian community by way of *koinōnia*, *diakonia*, and *kerygma*, the community feels the need of sending men forth to establish in other places new communities that are brought together by the Spirit through the word.

A primary distinction (leaving unity unimpaired) therefore arises between those who carry out the mission by "diffusion"—that is, by involving themselves in the human group to which they belong and in its problems, aspirations, and struggles—and those who are sent, in virtue of the same inner dynamism, to incorporate themselves in another human community and even in a different geographical and sociocultural milieu.

Further distinctions can also arise among the members of the community: among those who remain or among those who have been sent. Mission, after all, develops in the form of witness, communion, service, and preaching. Each individual therefore, according to the needs he faces, his personal outlook and aspirations, and the invitations given him by the community, can—and in concrete circumstances must—stress one or other of these several dimensions of mission. The Church already has various models of missionary existence: lay missionaries, religious missionaries, priest missionaries; and it has various groups which unite people of similar vocation: religious institutes, secular institutes, sacerdotal institutes. Other models and groups are possible; they may be required by the historical situation and brought into being by the Spirit. To make a choice of model or group on the basis of the universal call to the *ekklesia* and its mission is the business of each individual. He must listen to the voice of the Spirit, consult his community, discern the signs of the times, the concrete needs he sees, and his own circumstances, and evaluate his personal abilities and attitudes.

The most important and, admittedly, the most difficult thing to achieve is to make sure that every choice is grounded in a total and constantly revived openness to the Spirit and, at the same time, in a realistic outlook which does not seek refuge from history and from the responsibilities which Christ entrusts to us there for the full liberation of mankind.

We need only add that a genuine professional qualification may be far more important today than an accumulation of "consecrations" and of names and memberships. This kind of qualification implies the development of all the abilities God has given us and all the talents he has entrusted to us. The missionary will be truly a missionary to the extent that he works effectively for both the material and the spiritual good of the people with whom he is involved.

CONCLUSION

THE MISSIONARY CHURCH
CONFESSES BELIEF IN ITS
CRUCIFIED LORD

*What is the authentic Church of Christ?
Only the Church which accepts and con-
fesses belief in him as crucified, today, in
the poor and persecuted and oppressed of
our world.*

The language of the cross is an elementary
kind of language, but it is difficult to grasp, as
all simple things are. Let us lay hold of the cross
and remove it from the sacral scenery within
which we are accustomed to see it: candles,
flowers, and altars. Let us remove it, for a
moment, even from the context of the resurrection. Let us keep only the inscription: "Jesus of
Nazareth, king of the Jews," with its irony that
borders on comedy. Let us think of the cross for
a moment as an isolated episode, apart from the
historical aftermath: Jesus of Nazareth, accused
of subverting the people and rebelling against
civil and religious authority, and eliminated
because he was a threat to public peace.

We ask spontaneously what the early community (model of our faith, and a community for which the Cross had not yet become an ornamental knick-knack) thought of the painful and unpleasant death of its Lord. An "ecclesial" page of Matthew's Gospel (16:13-28) gives us insight, I think, into the confrontation between the Church and the crucified Christ.

Here, as often, the evangelist shapes a catechetical unit out of various scenes or sequences from the life of Christ. The actors, however, are no longer primarily the contemporaries of the earthly Jesus; they are disciples of the risen Christ who lives on in the community through his Spirit. The experiences of the people portrayed here are those of the first community: at times full of enthusiasm for the following of the Master, at times weak and lethargic, cowardly and unfaithful. Among the disciples a figure of the first rank is Peter, considered to be the model disciple and the spokesman for the community.

Many pages of Matthew's Gospel are inspired by this ongoing dialogue between the risen Christ and his *ekklesia*. One of these pages, as we have indicated, is Matthew 16:13-28. Here we have a sequence which unfolds in three interrelated stages: (1) Peter's Messianic confession: vv. 13-19; (2) Jesus' Messianic profession: vv. 21-22; (3) an explanatory conclusion: vv. 23-28.

The first scene is the most attractive and best known. Jesus addresses to the representa-

114

tive of the Church the official, solemn question: What do I mean for you, when all is said and done? The answer comes quickly and is just as solemn: You are the Christ, the Son of the living God; you are our Lord. Jesus answers by assuring them that the faith, which has been expressed by Peter and is, as it were, concentrated in his person, is firm and well-grounded, as immovable and lasting as rock, for it is based on the fidelity of God's own word. No destructive power will erode it.

Up to this point everything is fine. On the basis of this first scene the "Christ conquers, Christ rules, Christ, forever Lord!" has been chanted, declaimed, set to music, trumpeted forth, and written in huge letters on the walls of sanctuaries. But this path may well lead to the image of a Christ who is the abstract embodiment of spiritual power (and all that goes with it), while the administration of this power is duly guaranteed, in a monopolistic way, by his earthly representative; in other words, a Christ who is turned into an "idol," an alienated and alienating manifestation of man's own powers. Even after the multiplication of the loaves, his own followers wanted to make of him the kind of king they liked. So did Satan in the desert. Yet the only attribution of kingship which Christ accepted without protest was the one they nailed to the cross with him. Christ, Son of the living God, wants to be believed in as the kind of Messiah *he* is willing to be, not the kind we want.

The second scene in the sequence therefore brings a correction and explanation to the first. Jesus addresses to the Church his own carefully worded confession (or counterconfession): "From then on Jesus started to indicate to his disciples that he must go to Jerusalem and suffer greatly there at the hands of the leaders, the chief priests, and the scribes, and to be put to death, and raised up on the third day." The picture is clear: a direct and unswerving route to Jerusalem, the center of power; a speech (and a silence), just as direct, before the judgment seats of the Sanhedrin, Annas and Caiphas, Pilate, and Herod; a legal condemnation and just as legal an execution of it by a human justice from which there is no appeal; the cross and, only through the cross, the resurrection on the third day.

Peter and the other disciples knew what Christ meant. Their reaction—expressed once again by Peter—is quite different from what it was in the first scene. "May you be spared, Master! God forbid that any such thing should ever happen to you!" The hint of irony in the evangelist's account gives a tone of bitterness to this answer, otherwise so parallel to Peter's Messianic confession.

It must be added that this scene has not become as celebrated in Christian tradition as the first. It has been less frequently the topic of exegetical and theological study, of definitions and bulls, less often transcribed on the entablature of churches. Perhaps for this very reason it leaps across the barriers of time and space and, with the full power of him who spoke the words, pierces through our unhearing ears: "G out of my sight, you Satan! You are trying to make me trip and fall. You are not judging by God's standards but by man's."

It is easy for the Church to confess its faith in the glorious Messiah; it is difficult to declare oneself a disciple of the crucified Christ. This has been true from the very beginning. Therefore the evangelist insists on the point: "If a man wishes to come after me [Matthean language for "be a disciple of Christ"], he must deny his very self, take up his cross, and begin to follow in my footsteps. Whoever would save his life will lose it, but whoever loses his life for my sake will find it. [Here we would like Christ to add: I am well aware that existence is the most precious possession we have, far more precious than any other good.] What profit would a man show if he were to gain the whole world and destroy himself in the process? What can a man offer in exchange for his very self?"

Once again, the discourse is addressed primarily to the ecclesial community. The latter is confronted with the unqualified good which the "following of Christ" represents, with belonging to Christ, or, in other words, its identity as Church of Christ. Jesus says clearly and simply: There is no comparison between the goods of this world and the blessing of existence itself; the blessing of existence far outweighs all else. Well then, if you want to follow me, you must risk life itself. For no good, not even existence itself, can compare with belonging to Christ as his authentic Church. You cannot serve God and mammon. You cannot serve God and yourself.

To follow Christ means that the Church must deny itself and be disposed constantly to question its every structure, its every strategy and tactic, its every program and rule, in order to be free to choose, always and only, the line of thought and action proper to the crucified Christ.

The choice could not be more radical. On the one hand, the choice of the crucified Christ, with the possibility of being "his" Church; on the other, everything else, even survival. Everything is risked: rights, possessions, structures, relationships, alliances, even survival.

Is this not the paradox of Christian freedom? The existence of Christ's true Church is bound up with its poverty and freedom to follow its Master along the paths he has trodden; to seek him where he is, on the road to Golgotha; to follow him along that road, because only by losing one's life does one find it. There can be no clearer choice, no more all-embracing alternatives.

118

Things could not be otherwise, if it be true that Christ is *the* Word of God, the definitive, eschatological offering which God makes to man. The saving reality which is present to men in Christ, the kingdom which he inaugurates, is something qualitatively "other" and cannot be compared with the goods of this world. The qualitative difference and transcendence of the former makes it impossible to weigh them in a common scale. Christ's demands cannot but be unqualified. The choices he offers cannot be simply strategic short-term choices. They are, in the deepest sense, choices made against the grain. They can be made always and only, and unconditionally, with him as the crucified one; always and only as we follow his ways.

It would be a great illusion to think that we can genuinely encounter the crucified Christ, in all his brutal and discomfiting reality, in the often lifeless and stylized, artificial and illusory atmosphere of cult and liturgy. This is why he who said: "This is my body and my blood" added no less forcefully: "Whatever you did to the least . . . you did to me. . . . I was hungry and thirsty, and you satisfied (or did not satisfy) my need." There is no doubt that, for the evangelist, endeavoring to follow, always and only, the crucified Christ means, first of all and above all, endeavoring to follow, always and only, the poor, the weak, the helpless, the oppressed. The true future of the Church is

119

traced out by Christ's journey towards the human calvaries, the human areas where men are crucified. Its sole objective, which always lies ahead of us, must be to follow Christ along the roads he travels, attentive always not to confuse him with the pseudo-messiahs, but to seek him out on the roads where he is truly to be found, and to encounter him where he truly manifests his presence. On this continuous following of Christ the Church's authentic survival depends; its true life is bound up with the total and exclusive choice of the crucified Christ.

We must, then, follow *his* paths, frequent *his* milieus, unite with *his* friends, prefer *his* kind of people. For, when he comes for the last time (as the final verses of Matt. 16 say he will), the only question he will ask his Church is whether it has learned to follow him and encounter him and find him where he is. Has it learned to meet him on the path of suffering: the paths of poor and oppressed mankind, the crossing where the byways meet, the most destitute quarters where men live, the human ghettos of every kind, the camps where the offscourings of society live their marginal existence; wherever there is persecution and oppression; wherever, in a word, he has gone and continues to go, taking up his cross?

All this the Church is to do in a clear and consistent way, calling a spade a spade, as he did. All this the Church must say to small and great, even if it means being dragged before the judgment seats of this world's Caiphases and Pilates and allowing human justice to take its course. It must remember that whenever the choices of Christ's disciples are not straightforward, simple, and unequivocal, in favor of the poor and oppressed against the rich and the oppressor, the Church automatically becomes a Satan. The rhythm of faith in Christ is restless and upsetting, just as his own life was. But he has told us that *this* faith is the only faith that overcomes the world. It is the only faith that can challenge and liberate, because it is the explosive reaction to a logic of relationships based on selfishness and exploitation, and because it offers in a concrete way an alternative logic of fellowship, according to which it is "better to give than to receive," even where what is given is life itself.

The Church will be saved only if it seeks out and pursues the poor, choosing and coopting them as the privileged citizens of the kingdom. They are the Church's only salvation. Paradoxically (but the whole Gospel message is a paradox) we must say that only until the crucified Christ comes—in the countries said to be in process of development (it would be more accurate to say: in process of underdevelopment), as well as everywhere else—does the Church have the possibility and hope of survival. In this radical and fully evangelical sense only a

Church that is missionary to the marrow of its bones can be the Church of the crucified Christ. The mission of the Church, today more than ever before, must be studied, programmed, and carried out with the concentrated sense of urgency characteristic of men who, existing as they do in the eschatological situation between the first and second comings of the Son, are aware of the critical importance of the time and know that the Son may come at any moment to ask an account of their own choices and actions. Such a sense of mission can and must mark the Church, restoring vitality and assuring increase to the ecclesial communities, and preventing the Church from becoming the tasteless salt that is good for nothing but to be trodden under foot.

Christ promises the solidity of the rock and a victory over the negative and oppressive forces that rule this world, but he promises these to *this Church of his*: the Church that has the courage to live wholly and solely an outgoing, missionary existence and to move out in an active, intelligent way to the poor and to the crucified and bloody Christ of our day.

NOTES

[1] This passage appears as an exergue in the Italian version of Ernst Bloch's *Atheism in Christianity* (*Ateismo nel cristianesimo* [Milan: Feltrinelli, 1971]).

[2] In speaking of man as free, we do not deny that his freedom is not complete and total, that it is not fully human, that it does not reach the most interior and personal levels of his being. The full flowering of freedom coincides with the full maturing of the personality; such maturity in turn is an attribute primarily of the personal levels of man, for it implies an independence from every power that is not the totally free and liberating power of God (that is, the Spirit of God). The prototypical person in whom Christian poverty and freedom are ideally realized is the Virgin Mother, who is the poorest and freest of all God's creatures. She therefore provides the ideal human context for the manifestation of the Spirit, for in her the Spirit was able to effect his greatest, his unsurpassable miracle: Christ; and in her the Father was able to speak his clearest and most decisive word of salvation to men: his own Word.

Poverty is closely connected with Christian freedom. "Poverty" means, first and foremost (first in importance, not in time), an interior poverty. This in turn is the expression of basic choice of the God of freedom and the Exodus; since that choice is basic and exclusive, it is in the highest degree liberating.

[3] It is difficult to understand why this passage, which Old Testament scholars agree is a unit even from a literary point of view, should be shortened in the liturgy, where verses 11-15 are omitted, thus lessening the meaning and effectiveness of the whole composition. Cf. first reading for Tuesday of second week of Lent. [But, n.b., the whole section is used as first reading for Monday of the fifteenth week of the year (Year II).—Tr.]

[4] The following oracles of Isaiah may suitably be read in the present context: Isa. 3:12-15: Yahweh defends the poor man against the political leaders who try to justify their oppressive use of power by appealing to the authority of God; Isa. 5:8-9: against rich oppressors; Isa. 9:7-20: against the brother who devours his brother; Isa. 10:1-4: against those who make laws for their own advantage against the poor; Isa. 28:7-22: against the priests and officially recognized prophets who oppose Yahweh's prophet when he defends the poor.

[5] Religious institutes (missionary or not) should have the courage and honesty to face up to such accusations and ask themselves: how much time, money, activity, energy, life, books, and study do their members give to preparation for action that will liberate men? In the light of the preoccupations of the God of the Bible, isn't it odd that, for example, a student in a missionary group will spend so much time studying theology but not bother at all about preparing for activity of a social nature?

[6] Jürgen Moltmann, *Theology of Hope: On the Ground and the Implications of a Christian Eschatology,* tr. by James W. Leitch (New York: Harper & Row, 1967), pp. 27-28.

[7] The reference is to the first missionary sermon of

Peter after the Spirit's descent; he proclaims the fulfillment of Joel's prophecy which foresaw the outpouring of the Lord's Spirit upon every man in the last days.

[8] We are thinking of the missionary institutes. If they are to express in a more perfect way the mission of Christ, they must bear in mind the areas where they are to work, and take care to prepare their members in such a way that they can respond to some particular kind of human need (for such needs should find a saving response based on the Gospel). Christ, the Savior of the world, can require of anyone with an authentic missionary vocation a professional preparation and qualification in the medical field or the socio-political, or the technical-agricultural, etc.

[9] Cf. Johannes B. Metz, *Theology of the World,* tr. by William Glen-Doepel (New York: Herder and Herder, 1969), p. 50, n. 51: "The Church must be understood within the framework of the universal will of God for the world. God is concerned with the world, not really with the Church as different from the world. Only because the loving acceptance of the world by God was rejected and protested by the world did the 'Church' come into being at all (as distinct from the 'world')—as a sign and guarantee of the ultimate victory of God in relation to the world, which resisted him and, falling victim to itself in sin, also missed finding its own being. Hence the Church must always *also* be seen as that provisional thing that it is in salvation history (and which finally falls back again on the world itself)."

[10] Cf. Gualberto Gualerni, *La dinamica del rinnovamento ecclesiale* (Bologna: Edizioni Dehoniane, 1972), pp. 31-32.

[11] Cf. Metz, *Theology of the World,* pp. 53-54.

[12] Cf. Juan Alfaro, *Speranza cristiana e liberazione dell'uomo* (Brescia: Queriniana, 1972).

[13] Edward Schillebeeckx, O.P., "La condizione del cristiano nella civiltà secolare," in *La chiese provocata dal mondo* (Brescia: Queriniana, 1971), pp. 47-48. —If what Schillebeeckx says is true, then so is this other statement of Jürgen Moltman in his *Religion, Revolution, and the Future*, tr. by M. Douglas Meeks (New York: Scribner's, 1969), p. 69: "Therefore, Christian freedom is not a special one, different from that freedom for which all mankind is longing. Nor is it a partial one that is exhausted in the practice of a certain religion or cult. If it really is the beginning of the realm of freedom in the midst of all the misery of this world, then Christians can only demonstrate this freedom by using their own freedom for actual liberation of man from his real misery."

[14] Edward Schillebeeckx, O.P., *The Mission of the Church* (New York: Seabury, 1973). (Rome: Edizioni Paoline, 1971).

[15] Cf. Joseph Ratzinger, *Vorlesungen über Grundzüge der Ekklesiologie* (mimeographed notes for a course on ecclesiology at the University of Tübingen, 1968-69), pp. 88-89.

[16] We are concerned here only with the missionary sermons addressed to Jews. Acts contains two missionary sermons addressed to pagans (14:15-17; 17:16-32); both are by Paul, and their pattern and content are different from those of the sermons we are studying here.

[17] Cf. Alfaro, *op. cit.*, p. 152: "Through the gift of the Spirit all mankind is called to share the glory of the risen Christ, not simply in spiritual inwardness but in the body as well."

[18] Cf. Francis X. Durrwell, *The Mystery of Christ and the Apostolate,* tr. by Edward Quinn (New York: Sheed & Ward, 1972), pp. 66-91; Hans Küng, "What Is the Essence of Apostolic Succession?" in Hans Küng (ed.), *Apostolic Succession: Rethinking a Barrier to Unity (Concilium* 34; New York: Paulist Press, 1968), pp. 28-35.

[19] Schillebeeckx, "La condizione del cristiano . . . ," pp. 55-56.

[20] Karl Rahner, "La nuova immagine della Chiesa," in *La chiesa provocata dal mondo,* p. 8.

[21] Johannes B. Metz, "The Church and the World," in T. Patrick Burke (ed.), *The Word in History* (New York: Sheed & Ward, 1966), pp. 81-82.